HAL LEONARD
GUITAR
MUSIC THEORY

Written by Chad Johnson

Contributing Editor: Eric Wills

2 INTRODUCTION
How to Use This Book,
Recommended Practice Schedule

3 THE BASICS
Tab Review, Rhythm Review, Fretboard Diagram

6 INTERVALS: PART 1
What Is an Interval?, Half Steps, Whole Steps

9 THE MUSICAL ALPHABET
Sharps and Flats, Natural Half Steps

11 CHECKPOINT 1
Note Names, Musical Terms, Intervals
and the Musical Alphabet

12 INTERVALS: PART 2
Interval Quantity, Interval Quality, Interval Shapes

19 CHECKPOINT 2
Interval Quantity, Interval Quality, Interval Shapes,
Musical Terms

21 THE MAJOR SCALE
Intervallic Formula, Major Scale Patterns,
Major Scale Chart

25 CHORDS: PART 1
Triads, Chord Voicings, Harmonizing the Major Scale,
The Harmonized Major Scale Formula,

29 CHECKPOINT 3
Triads, Harmonized Major Scale, Musical Terms

30 CHORDS: PART 2
Transposing Chord Progressions

37 THE MINOR SCALE
The Numeric Formula, Essential Minor Scale
Patterns, Harmonizing the Minor Scale, Minor Chord
Progressions, The V–I Cadence

42 THE MINOR DOMINANT CHORD

43 BEYOND TRIADS
The Numeric Code, Seventh Chords,
Suspended Chords

46 APPENDIX
Checkpoint Answer Keys

To access audio visit:
www.halleonard.com/mylibrary

Enter Code
6163-8712-5823-2526

ISBN 978-1-4950-2901-1

7777 W. BLUEMOUND RD. P.O. BOX 13819 MILWAUKEE, WI 53213

Visit Hal Leonard Online at
www.halleonard.com

INTRODUCTION

This method is designed to be used with electric or acoustic guitar. As long as the guitar is in standard tuning, all of this information is equally applicable to either. This book is not a beginning method; rather it should be thought of as a supplement. As such, it's assumed that you already have some familiarity with the instrument and have worked on basic skills, such as playing chords and single notes. However, it's never too early to start learning music theory, so we won't assume much beyond that.

 If you don't have access to a tuner, you can find tuning pitches on the accompanying audio (see page 1 for directions on how to access the audio tracks).

HOW TO USE THIS BOOK

Music theory is a language, much like English or Spanish. It deals with conventions, names, and formulas that help to explain how music works. Therefore, it's important that you understand a topic before you move on to the next, as each new section will build upon previously covered material. In order to make the learning as fun as possible, we'll use riffs and excerpts from real songs to help illustrate the concepts. However, simply playing through these will hardly teach you a thing if you skip over the material that precedes them.

All of this is to say that you need to work through this book from front to back—without skipping—in order to receive the greatest benefit. If you feel the desire to skip ahead because you think you already know something, I advise you to reconsider and simply consider the section a review. There's always the chance that you'll discover something you didn't know and/or additional light will be shed on a topic that will help broaden your overall understanding. At the very least, you should skim ahead until you find something that's unfamiliar to you (but a review never hurt anyone!).

RECOMMENDED PRACTICE SCHEDULE

You may have heard that it's better to practice every day for 30 minutes than it is to practice for four hours on a Sunday once a week. That's definitely good advice, and the same applies to the learning of music theory. The information is best learned in smaller, daily doses than in one extended, super-long session. It's important to give your brain time to assimilate and process the new information, and much of this activity actually takes place behind the scenes, when you're not even consciously thinking about it. (It's the same idea as trying to remember the name of a song or movie; after you give up, a few days later it will just pop into your head because your brain was still working on the problem behind the scenes.)

You can cram for a history test in one night and maybe even retain the information long enough to get a good grade the next day, but chances are, you'll forget just about everything shortly thereafter. By the same token, if you want to learn music theory for good, you need to work on it on a regular basis and allow yourself time to properly digest the information.

I recommend allotting a percentage of your daily practice time to working through this book. If you have, say, an hour scheduled to practice, you might set aside 15 or 20 minutes of that time for theory. Take all the time you need, making sure you fully understand the concepts being taught before moving on. If you're working through more than one section a day, I'd suggest that you're probably progressing too quickly.

THE BASICS

Now that you're in tune and ready to go, let's get started. We'll begin with a quick review of some essential concepts to make sure that we're all up to speed before we tackle the more heady stuff.

TAB REVIEW

In this book, we'll use a system of guitar notation called **tablature**, or "**tab**." In case you're not yet familiar with this system, here's a quick review:

The tab staff contains six lines—one for each string of the guitar. The thickest string (the low E, or sixth string) is on the bottom, and the thinnest (high E, or first string) is on the top, so it looks the same as when you're looking down at the neck from playing position.

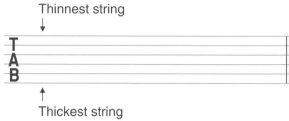

Numbers on the lines indicate which frets you should play on each string. Just as with text, we read the notes from left to right. A "0" indicates the string is to be played "open," or unfretted. In the following staff, the low E string is first played open and then at the first fret.

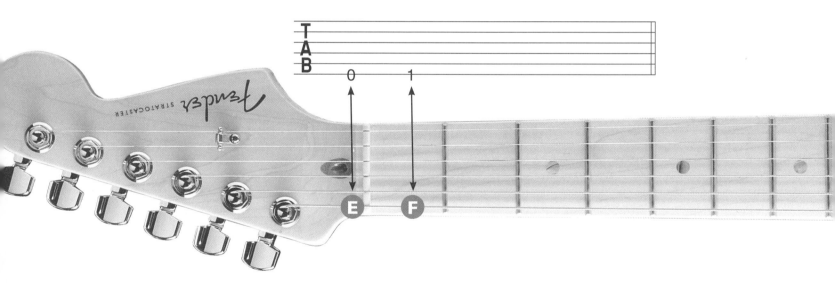

When notes are stacked on top of each other, they should be played simultaneously. In the following example, you would first play the open fifth string and the fourth string, second fret together. Then you would play the sixth string, third fret and the fifth string, fifth fret together.

The notes on the guitar neck make up only half the picture, though. By looking at the tab examples above, we still don't know how the song is supposed to sound because we don't have all the necessary information. The other important element is the **rhythm** of the notes that we play.

RHYTHM REVIEW

If you've never read standard music before, that's OK; you can still use this book. But you will need to learn how to read rhythms before we go any further in order to play the examples.

Music is broken up into **measures**, or **bars**, using **bar lines** to make it easier to keep your place. (Imagine trying to read a book with no paragraph breaks.) The **time signature** at the beginning of a piece of music tells you how the music is counted and how the measures are divided. The top number of the time signature tells you how many beats are in a measure, and the bottom number tells you what type of note is counted as one beat. The most common time signature in rock and pop music is 4/4, which tells you that there are four beats in a measure (top number), and the quarter note (1/4) is counted as one beat.

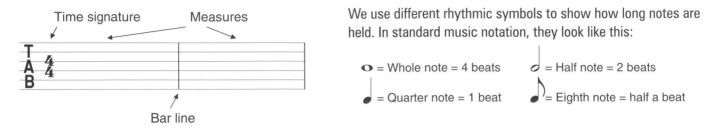

We use different rhythmic symbols to show how long notes are held. In standard music notation, they look like this:

𝅝 = Whole note = 4 beats   𝅗𝅥 = Half note = 2 beats

♩ = Quarter note = 1 beat   ♪ = Eighth note = half a beat

In this book, we're using **rhythm tab** instead of standard notation, which combines tablature with rhythmic symbols. So this is what the same rhythmic values above would look like in rhythm tab:

Note that, when there are several eighth notes in a row, a **beam** will connect the stems, like this:

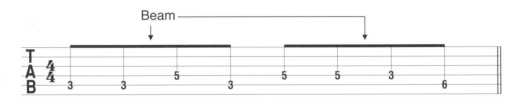

There are also symbols that tell you when to stop playing. These are called **rests**:

▬ = Whole rest = 4 beats   ▬ = Half rest = 2 beats   𝄽 = Quarter rest = 1 beat   𝄾 = Eighth rest = half a beat

Listen to the audio for this example and try to count along with the rhythms to make sure you understand them before moving on. When counting eighth notes, add an "and" in between the beats: "1-and, 2-and," etc. Once you can count it, try playing along while counting.

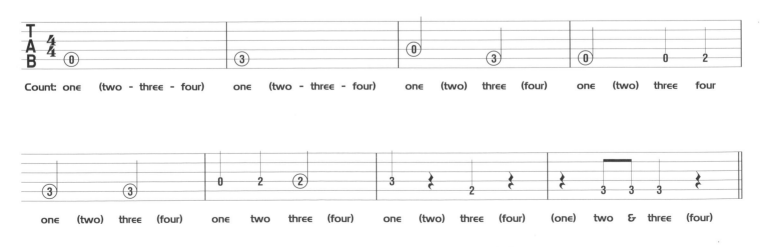

FRETBOARD DIAGRAM

In order to understand the concepts on which music theory is based, you'll need to be able to identify the notes on the guitar neck. Therefore, the following neck diagram is presented as a reference. Notice that, after fret 12, the order begins all over again. In other words, frets 0–11 contain the same notes as frets 12–23 (if your guitar has 24 frets).

F		F#/Gb	G	G#/Ab	A	A#/Bb	B	C	C#/Db	D	D#/Eb	E	F	F#/Gb	G
C		C#/Db	D	D#/Eb	E	F	F#/Gb	G	G#/Ab	A	A#/Bb	B	C	C#/Db	D
G#/Ab		A	A#/Bb	B	C	C#/Db	D	D#/Eb	E	F	F#/Gb	G	G#/Ab	A	A#/Bb
D#/Eb		E	F	F#/Gb	G	G#/Ab	A	A#/Bb	B	C	C#/Db	D	D#/Eb	E	F
A#/Bb		B	C	C#/Db	D	D#/Eb	E	F	F#/Gb	G	G#/Ab	A	A#/Bb	B	C
F		F#/Gb	G	G#/Ab	A	A#/Bb	B	C	C#/Db	D	D#/Eb	E	F	F#/Gb	G

↑
Fret 12

TWO FRETS UP, TWO STRINGS OVER

It's not imperative (or expected) that you memorize the entire fretboard right now. You can flip back to this page as needed while working through the book. However, it's certainly advisable that you learn all the notes as soon as you can. Working through this book will no doubt help with this task, but there are a few other tricks that help, as well. One is the "two frets up, two strings over" trick.

If you take a look at the notes on string 6, you'll notice that the notes on string 4 are the same, only two frets higher. These notes are one **octave** apart. The two notes of the octave share the same letter name and sound very much alike, except one is higher and the other is lower in pitch.

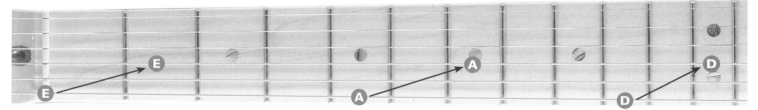

The same idea works for strings 5 and 3, as well.

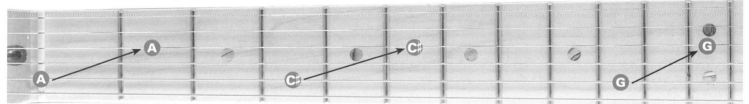

So, this means that, once you learn the notes along string 6, learning them on string 4 will go pretty quickly. The same can be said for strings 5 and 3.

Also, since both the sixth and first strings are tuned to the note E, the notes along those strings will have the same names. The notes on these two strings are two octaves apart.

TWO FRETS DOWN, THREE STRINGS OVER

To learn the notes on string 2 easily, you can use the "two frets down, three strings over" trick. In other words, the notes on string 5 will have the same names as the notes on string 2, only two frets lower. These notes are one octave apart.

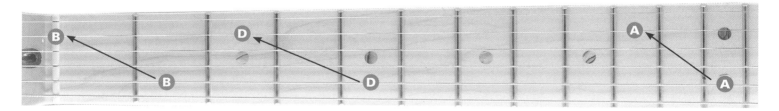

Go ahead and dog-ear this page so you can quickly flip back to it as needed in the early stages of your studies.

INTERVALS: PART 1

If there's one concept that lies at the heart of practically all things music theory, it's the interval. So that's where we'll begin.

WHAT IS AN INTERVAL?

An **interval** can be described as the musical distance between notes. It simply measures how far away, in pitch, notes are from each other.

Intervals help us define scales, chords, and just about every element of harmony. They're usually counted with half steps and whole steps, so let's talk about those.

HALF STEPS

A **half step** is the distance of one fret (on the same string) on the guitar. It's the smallest interval possible in our Western musical system. It's also the distance from one key to the very next—black or white—on a piano keyboard. All the intervals shown below are half steps.

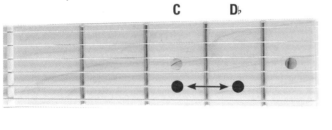
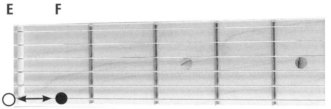

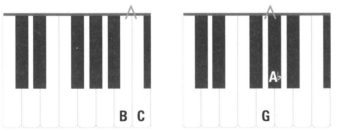

You may ask why we're looking at a piano keyboard. Well, whereas the guitar fretboard looks the same all over (irrespective of the inlayed position markers), the piano makes an excellent visual reference when discussing intervals because of the presence of black and white keys. Therefore, we'll occasionally make use of the keyboard for visual aid.

METAL-APPROVED HALF STEPS 🔊 3))

Half steps are used all the time in music of all genres. They can sound very ominous when power chords are built from them. Here's a riff built from E5 and F5 power chords, which lay a half step away from each other.

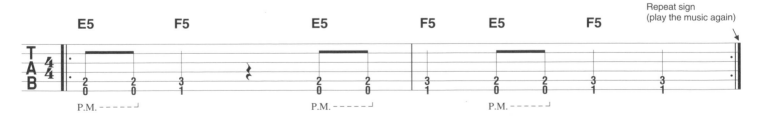

GOT SUSPENSE? 🔊4))

Repeating half steps is always a nice way to generate suspense. The dots under the F notes are called **staccato** markings. They tell you to play the note short and clipped.

WHOLE STEPS

A **whole step** is, as you may have guessed, twice the distance of a half step. In other words, it's the equivalent of two frets (on the same string) on the guitar and two keys (black or white) on the piano keyboard. All the intervals below are whole steps.

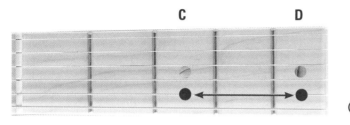

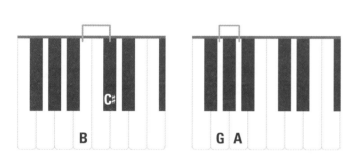

Compare the above intervals to those in the diagrams on page 6, and you'll find that each one is twice the size. Whole steps appear just as ubiquitously in music as half steps do.

WHOLE-STEP RIFF 🔊5))

Sometimes all you need is a whole step to create a great riff. Here, we're using only the notes C and D, which lay a whole step apart. At the end, we play the same two notes an octave higher. There's that "two frets up, two strings over" trick at work! The dashed curved line is a **tie**, which tells you to play the first note and sustain it through the value of the next.

BLUESY RIFF 6))

Whole steps can sound nice and bluesy, too, especially when you give the lower note a subtle quarter-step bend. The ($\sqcap$ = $\sqcap$) symbol tells you to play the eighth notes with a **shuffle feel**. This is a lopsided sound (the first eighth note in each beat lasts longer than the second) that's extremely popular in blues, jazz, and other styles as well.

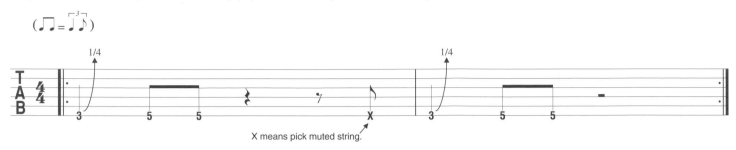

X means pick muted string.

BLUESY OCTAVE RIFF 7))

Here's another riff using whole steps an octave apart. This time, we're using the notes D and E.

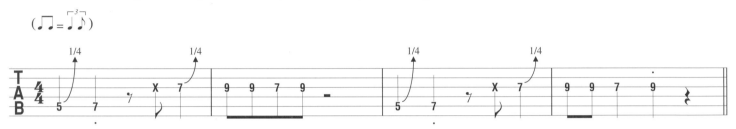

Let's take a look at some songs that make use of these intervals. Remember to check back with the fretboard diagram on page 5 when necessary to keep track of the note names.

YOU REALLY GOT ME 8))

The Kinks put the whole step to good use for the main riff to "You Really Got Me," which consists of power chords a whole step apart: F5 and G5.

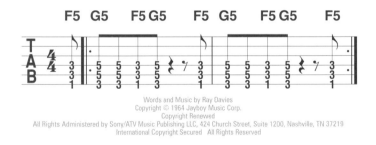

ROCKY MOUNTAIN WAY 9))

Joe Walsh used a whole-step chord movement to fuel one of the main riffs in his classic hit "Rocky Mountain Way." With the open low E string chugging away in between, he moves a D5 chord up a whole step to E5 in dramatic fashion.

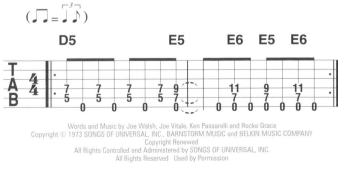

THE MUSICAL ALPHABET

Before we get too much further, we need to talk a bit about the **musical alphabet**. This is simply the term that refers to the note names that we use in music. The musical alphabet consists of the letters A through G. So, if you continue up past the note G, you start over again with A in the next octave. If you go down below the note A, you start again with G and continue down, etc.

On the guitar, an octave is the distance of 12 frets on the same string.

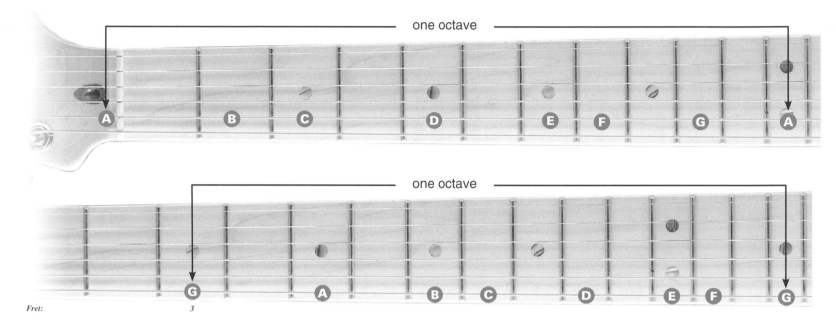

SHARPS & FLATS

Since there are 12 frets in an octave on the guitar, it makes sense that there are 12 different notes available to us, but we've only learned the names of seven (A through G). The remaining "in-between" notes are named using sharp and flat symbols.

- A **sharp** (♯) is a half step higher than a natural note.
- A **flat** (♭) is a half step lower than a natural note.

For example, the note directly higher than A is A♯ (read: "A-sharp"). The note directly lower than A is A♭ ("A-flat").

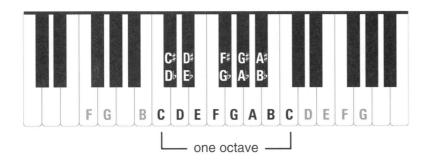

But wait a minute—the note that's a half step lower than A is also a half step higher than G. So couldn't it be called G♯? Yes, it can! It can actually be named either of these; it all depends on the musical context. The term for this—when the same note has two different names—is **enharmonic**. So we say that G♯ and A♭ are enharmonic to each other.

Refer back to the fretboard diagram on page 5 to see all of these enharmonic names on the guitar (indicated with the slash between the two letters).

On the piano, the regular, or "natural," notes are found on the white keys. All the black keys are sharps and flats. This is why it can be so helpful to look at a piano keyboard to visualize the relationship of notes.

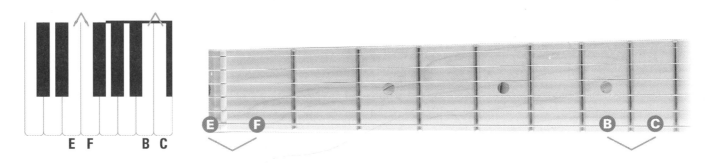

You have probably noticed that each "in-between" note has two possible names. How we decide to name the note (sharp vs. flat) can depend on the direction of the musical line, the key of the song it appears in, or other factors. For example, C-sharp and D-flat are the same pitch. The only difference is in how we decide it should be "spelled" within the context of a piece of music.

NATURAL HALF STEPS

When looking at the piano keyboard, you may have noticed that, while there are 12 different notes within an octave, seven keys are white and only five are black. This means that there are two places where white keys lay directly next to each other. These are the **natural half steps**: from B to C and from E to F.

So, does this mean that there's no such thing as a B♯, C♭, E♯, or F♭? Well, not necessarily. Those note names are not nearly as common as all the other sharps and flats, but they will pop up in certain musical contexts. What's important to remember is that, while A to B (or G to A, D to E, etc.) is a whole step, the distance from B to C and from E to F is only a half step. And this is why the piano keyboard is so helpful in this regard.

This information will be important when we learn how to build scales from different root notes. The **root** (also known as the **tonic**) is the note that sounds like home. It's the note after which the **key** of the song is named. So, if we say a song is in the "key of G," then G is the root.

CHECKPOINT I

Before we move on any further, let's take a moment to review what we've learned so far. (You can check your answers to this quiz in the Appendix at the back of the book.)

NOTE NAMES

Identify the notes shown on these neck diagrams (you can reference page 5 if you don't have them memorized yet).

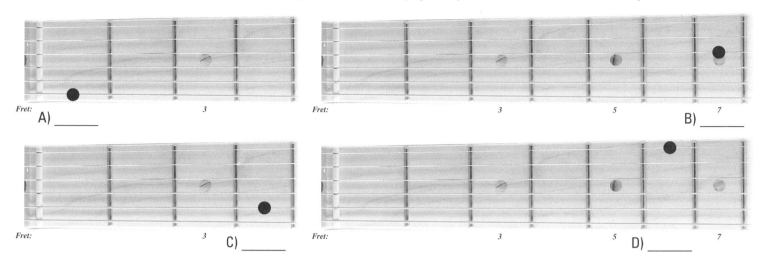

Fret: 3   A) _____

Fret: 3   5   B) _____ 7

Fret: 3   C) _____

Fret: 3   5   D) _____ 7

MUSICAL TERMS

Match each term in the left column with the correct description on the right.

Staccato	The distance between one note and another higher or lower note with the same name
Tie	The musical distance between notes
Shuffle feel	One note having two different names
Enharmonic	Short and clipped
Interval	Divides the music on the staff into measures
Octave	A curved, dashed line joining the rhythmic values of two notes
Bar line	An indication to play eighth notes in a lopsided manner

INTERVALS AND THE MUSICAL ALPHABET

Which letters are used in the musical alphabet? _____

How many frets equal one half step on the guitar? _____

How many frets equal one whole step on the guitar? _____

Where do the natural half steps occur in the musical alphabet? Between ___ and ___, and also between ___ and ___.

What is the enharmonic name for the note A#? _____

Identify whether the intervals below are half steps or whole steps, circling the correct one.

A) **half step** or **whole step**?   B) **half step** or **whole step**?   C) **half step** or **whole step**?

Fret: 3   Fret: 3   Fret: 7   9

Referencing the diagram on page 5 as necessary, determine whether the following are half steps or whole steps.

D) A to B♭: half step or whole step   E) D to E: half step or whole step   F) B to C#: half step or whole step

G) F to G♭: half step or whole step

INTERVALS: PART 2

Now that we've learned a bit about intervals, it's time to expand our knowledge. Just as we don't use only dollars and fifty-cent pieces to create sums of money, we don't solely use half steps and whole steps to measure intervals. Another, more practical way of naming intervals exists.

In this system, we name intervals with two separate parts: a **quality** and a **quantity**. An example is *minor 3rd*; "minor" is the quality, and "3rd" is the quantity. The quantity is a bit easier to grasp, so we'll start with that first.

INTERVAL QUANTITY

The quantity of an interval is really pretty simple; it just boils down to counting letter names. You simply count up from one letter name to the second letter name, and that's your quantity. You don't have to worry about sharps, flats, or anything else—you just count letters. For example, if we want to know the quantity of the interval from C to F, we simply count:

C (1)   D (2)   E (3)   F (4)

So, from C up to F is a 4th.

What would be the quantity of the interval from D up to B?

D (1)   E (2)   F (3)   G (4)   A (5)   B (6)

The answer is a 6th.

That's really all there is to the quantity. If you want to measure an interval going down, it's the same process; you just count backwards through the musical alphabet. What would be the interval from D *down* to G?

D (1)   C (2)   B (3)   A (4)   G (5)

The answer is a 5th.

If counting backwards feels funny to you, however, then you can simply **invert** the interval and count *up* to get the same result. Instead of figuring out the interval from D down to G, for example, you can switch them and count from G *up* to D. You'll get the same result either way:

G (1)   A (2)   B (3)   C (4)   D (5)

So, from G *up* to D is a 5th, just as from D *down* to G was a 5th.

When you're figuring an interval's quantity while dealing with note names that include sharps and/or flats, you can simply remove all of the sharps or flats and just count the letters.

From C# to G♭:   C (1)   D (2)   E (3)   F (4)   G (5) = 5th

From E♭ to F#:   E (1)   F (2) = 2nd

However, even though the quantity tells us that from C# up to G♭ is some kind of 5th, it doesn't tell us specifically which kind of 5th it is. That's where the quality comes in, and we'll look at that next.

INTERVAL QUALITY

Now it's time to take a look at the other important part of the interval: the quality. For this, we'll once again be using half and whole steps. While the quantity tells us the number of note names involved in an interval, the quality tells us the number of half and/or whole steps involved. In other words, there's not just one kind of 3rd, 5th, or 6th, etc. They can each have different *qualities*, as well.

Let's take a look at a chart to help shed some light on this. For this demonstration, we'll measure all the intervals up from the note C throughout one octave:

Notes	Number of Half Steps	Interval Name	Abbreviation
C to C	0	Perfect unison	P1
C to D♭	1	Minor 2nd	m2
C to D	2	Major 2nd	M2
C to E♭	3	Minor 3rd	m3
C to E	4	Major 3rd	M3
C to F	5	Perfect 4th	P4
C to G♭	6	Diminished 5th	d5
C to G	7	Perfect 5th	P5
C to A♭	8	Minor 6th	m6
C to A	9	Major 6th	M6
C to B♭	10	Minor 7th	m7
C to B	11	Major 7th	M7
C to C	12	Perfect octave	P8

Listen to the following track to hear how these intervals sound in their **melodic form**—i.e., one note played after the other.

🔊 10))

```
      m2          M2          m3          M3          P4          d5
T
A
B   3    4     3    5     3    6     3    7     3    8     3    9


      P5          m6          M6          m7          M7          P8

    3    10    3    11    3    12    3    13    3    14    3    15
```

Note: We measured all of the above in half steps for consistency, but they could be expressed with whole steps, as well. For example, we could also say a major 3rd is two whole steps (same as four half steps), or we could say a perfect 5th is three-and-a-half (whole) steps (same as seven half steps).

If you noticed, we used only flats for the non-natural notes in the previous chart. But what happens when we use their enharmonic names? All the natural notes stay the same, but everything else changes.

Notes	Number of Half Steps	Interval Name	Abbreviation
C to C	0	Perfect unison	P1
C to C♯	1	Augmented unison	A1
C to D	2	Major 2nd	M2
C to D♯	3	Augmented 2nd	A2
C to E	4	Major 3rd	M3
C to F	5	Perfect 4th	P4
C to F♯	6	Augmented 4th	A4
C to G	7	Perfect 5th	P5
C to G♯	8	Augmented 5th	A5
C to A	9	Major 6th	M6
C to A♯	10	Augmented 6th	A6
C to B	11	Major 7th	M7
C to C	12	Perfect octave	P8

A new type of interval, "augmented," is introduced here, and from the chart, we can deduce that:

- An **augmented interval** is one half step larger than a major or perfect interval; for example, a major 2nd is two half steps, so an augmented 2nd is three half steps. A perfect 5th is seven half steps, so an augmented 5th is eight half steps.

But how can C to C♯ be called an augmented unison? It doesn't really make much sense to call two notes "unison" unless they're the same pitch, but you have to remember our quantity rule: the interval quantity is only concerned with counting letter names. And since only one letter name is involved in C and C♯, it can't be called a "minor 2nd"; therefore, it gets the name "augmented unison" because it's one half step larger than a perfect unison.

Just as the English language has many so-called "rules" that get broken all the time in conventional usage, music theory has these types of things, as well. You're never going to hear someone referring to an "augmented unison" outside of a textbook—and even then, it won't come up much. Depending on the musical context, the other augmented intervals (2nd, 4th, 5th, and 6th) will get used occasionally, but they're not nearly as common as the major, minor, and perfect intervals.

Well, that's enough talking for now. Let's look at how to play these intervals so we can hear what they sound like in a musical context.

INTERVAL SHAPES

Now that we've learned how to spell intervals and heard how they sound in the melodic form, let's look at how to play them in their **harmonic form**—i.e., both notes played simultaneously—on the guitar. For the purpose of learning these, we'll continue to use the note C as the base note for each, but we'll move it down to string 6, fret 8 in order to make playing all of the intervals possible.

For each one, you'll hear the notes played separately (melodic form) and then together (harmonic form). Learning to recognize these intervals by ear will greatly help you in being able to play what you hear without having to check it on your instrument first. Try to relate each interval to a melody that you already know. For example, a perfect 4th sounds like the first two notes of "Here Comes the Bride." A major 6th sounds like the "N" and "B" from the NBC jingle.

MINOR 2ND 11

From C to D♭ is a minor 2nd. This is quite a stretch at this spot on the guitar. Play C with your 4th finger and D♭ with your 1st.

```
T
A
B    4
     8
```

MAJOR 2ND 12

From C to D is a major 2nd.

```
T
A
B    5
     8
```

MINOR 3RD 13

From C to E♭ is a minor 3rd.

```
T
A
B    6
     8
```

MAJOR 3RD 14

From C to E is a major 3rd.

```
T
A
B    7
     8
```

PERFECT 4TH 15

From C to F is a perfect 4th.

```
T
A
B    8
     8
```

DIMINISHED 5TH 16

From C to G♭ is a diminished 5th.

```
T
A
B    9
     8
```

PERFECT 5TH 17

From C to G is a perfect 5th.

```
T
A
B    10
     8
```

MINOR 6TH 18

From C to A♭ is a minor 6th.

```
T
A
B    11
     8
```

MAJOR 6TH 19

From C to A is a major 6th.

```
T
A
B    7
     8
```

MINOR 7TH 20

From C to B♭ is a minor 7th.

```
T
A
B    8
     8
```

MAJOR 7TH 21

From C to B is a major 7th.

```
T
A
B    9
     8
```

PERFECT OCTAVE 22

From C to C is a perfect octave.

```
T
A
B    10
     8
```

As with many things on the guitar, there are other ways to play some of these intervals—especially the 5ths and 6ths—but this is a good starting point. Of course, we won't always be playing these intervals from a C note on string 6, so let's look at the generic shapes based off each string that are moveable to any root note. We'll use standard guitar chord grids for these. Again, there are other ways to play some of these intervals, but these shapes probably represent the most commonly used.

MINOR 2ND

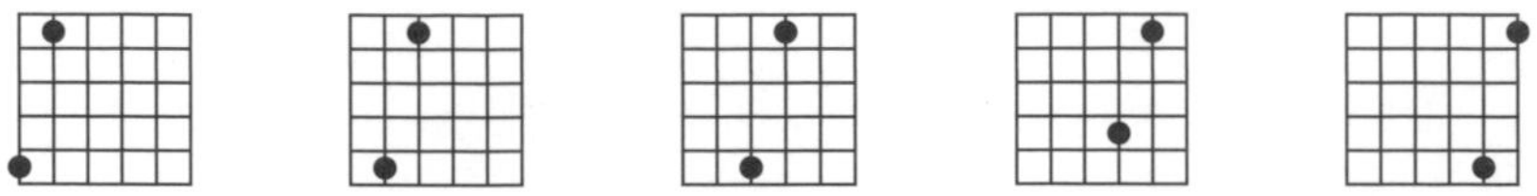

MAJOR 2ND

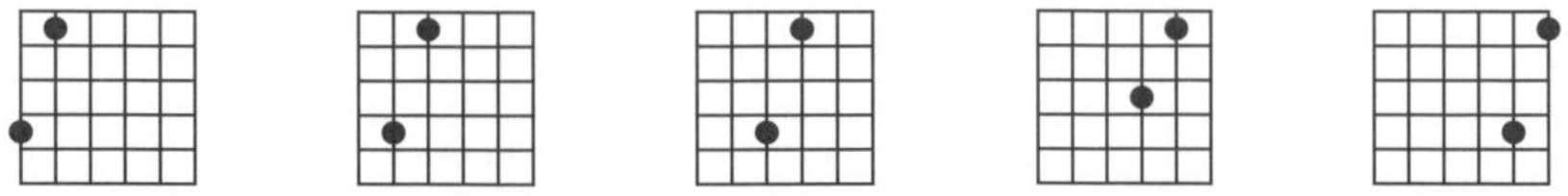

MINOR 3RD

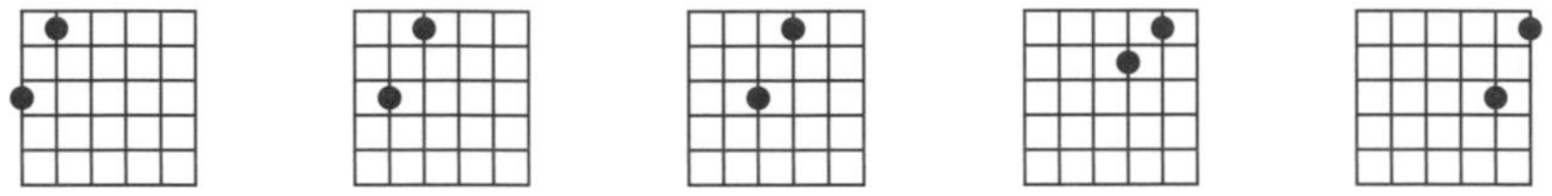

MAJOR 3RD

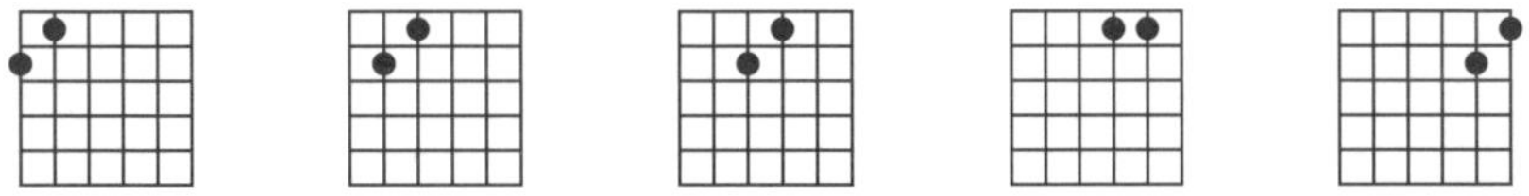

PERFECT 4TH

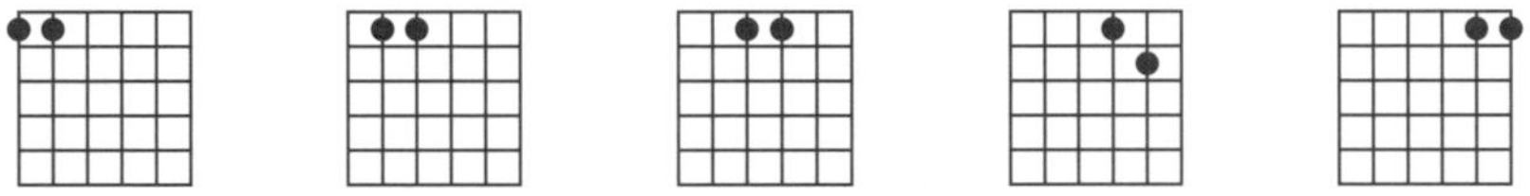

DIMINISHED 5TH

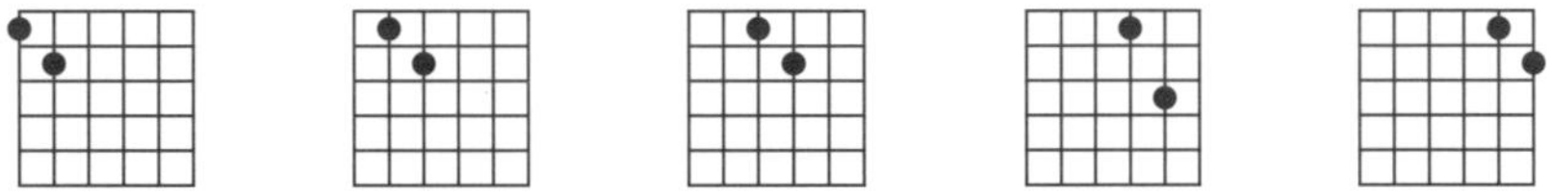

PERFECT 5TH

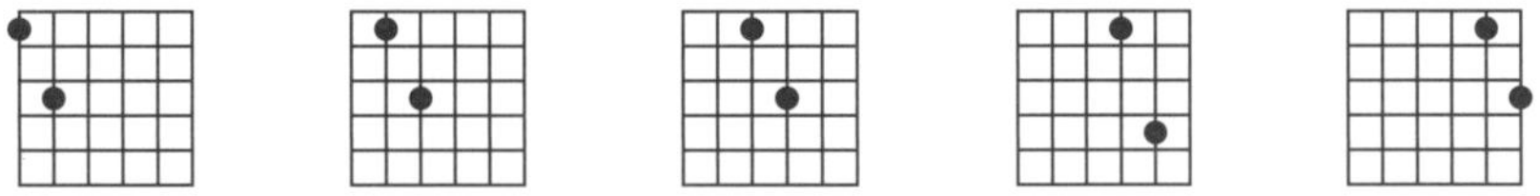

MINOR 6TH

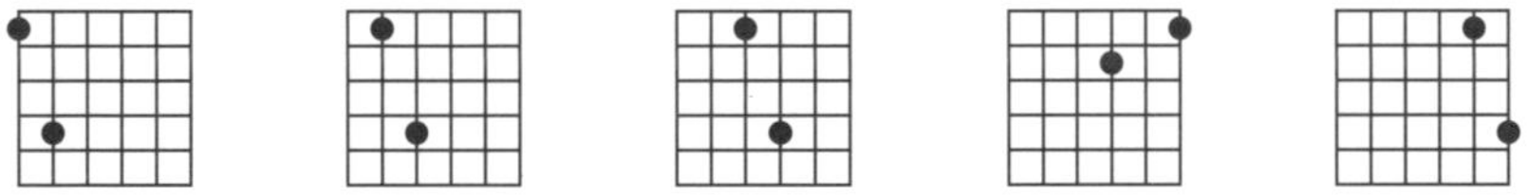

MAJOR 6TH

MINOR 7TH

MAJOR 7TH

PERFECT OCTAVE

Now that you've got all these interval shapes under your fingers, let's hear how some of them can be used to create great riffs.

ROCKIN' IN 5THS 23

The 5th interval is the one on which rock 'n' roll is largely built. There's nothing more powerful-sounding than a guitar playing 5ths. In fact, that's why it's called a **power chord**!

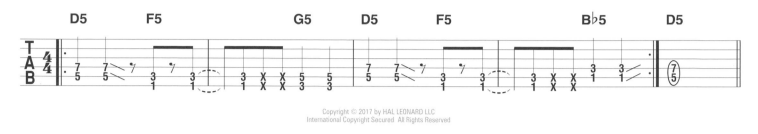

ROCKIN' IN 4THS 24

As it turns out, 4ths are the same as inverted 5ths. In other words, if we take a 5th—like C up to G—and then move the G note down an octave, we'll get a 4th: either C down to G or G up to C. Therefore, 4ths have a powerful sound that is similar to that of 5ths.

When a **dot** is added to a note, it increases its rhythmic value by 50 percent. So a dotted half note will last three beats instead of two. A dotted quarter note will last one-and-a-half beats instead of one, etc.

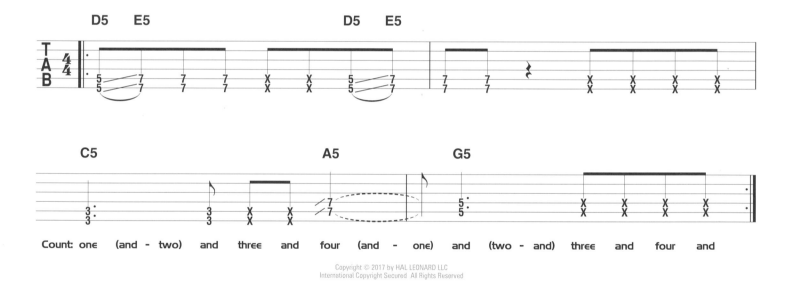

SMOKE ON THE WATER 25

By far the most common 4ths riff in rock history is Deep Purple's "Smoke on the Water."

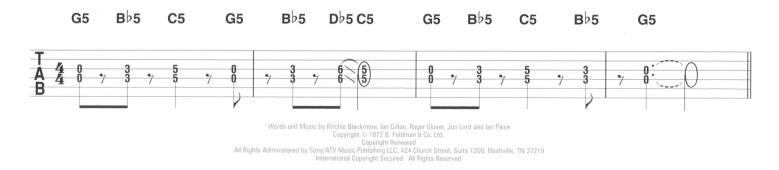

RUNNIN' WITH THE DEVIL 🔊 26))

Eddie Van Halen used a combination of major and minor 3rds on strings 4 and 3 for the verse riff in "Runnin' with the Devil." Note also that all of these appear over the open A string, creating a **pedal tone**—i.e., a tone that repeats while other tones change above or below it.

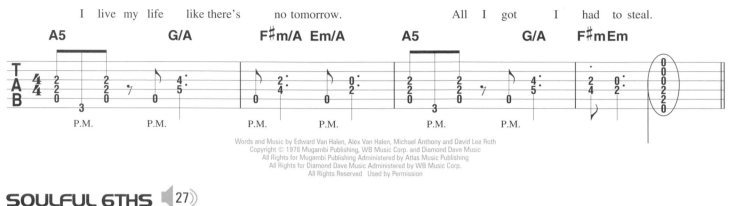

SOULFUL 6THS 🔊 27))

The 6th is a commonly featured interval in soul music guitar parts, as demonstrated here. This one is played with the fingers.

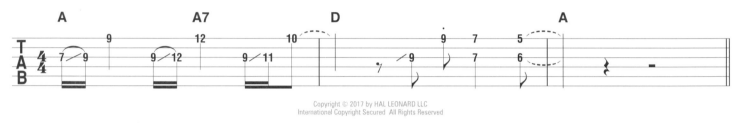

HIDE AWAY 🔊 28))

Blues players are also fond of the 6th. One of the most famous examples is this nimble-fingered classic riff from Freddie King's "Hide Away." This lick ends with a **triplet**, which divides a beat into three even eighth notes. You'll immediately recognize the sound.

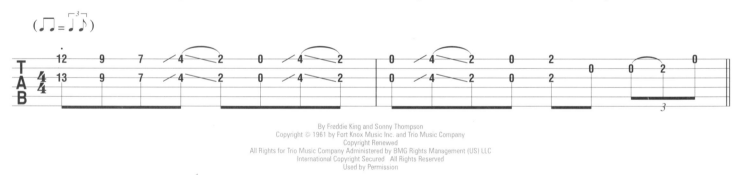

HELTER SKELTER 🔊 29))

The Beatles open their tour de force "Helter Skelter" with some grinding major 2nd intervals before relieving the tension slightly by moving to 3rds.

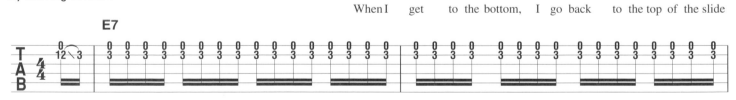

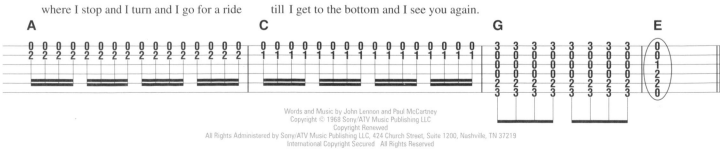

CHECKPOINT 2

Even though we're not halfway through the book, we've already done most of the really hard legwork. If you have a thorough understanding of intervals, then the rest of the music theory world should fall fairly nicely into place. From here on, we'll be working on things that are a bit more musical. But let's quickly review what we've learned thus far before we press on.

INTERVAL QUANTITY

Determine the correct interval quantity (3rd, 7th, etc.) of each pair of notes. Be sure to notice whether you're counting up or down. We're only looking for the quantity here!

1. From D up to G _____

2. From E♭ up to F♯ _____

3. From E down to G _____

4. From A♭ up to F♯ _____

5. From B♭ up to A _____

6. From C♯ down to B♭ _____

Name the missing note. Since we're only dealing with quantity, don't worry about adding any sharps or flats.

7. A 6th up from C is _____

8. A 5th up from E is _____

9. A 7th down from G is _____

10. A 4th down from B♭ is _____

11. A 2nd up from C♯ is _____

12. A 3rd up from D♭ is _____

Determine only the interval quantity in the following:

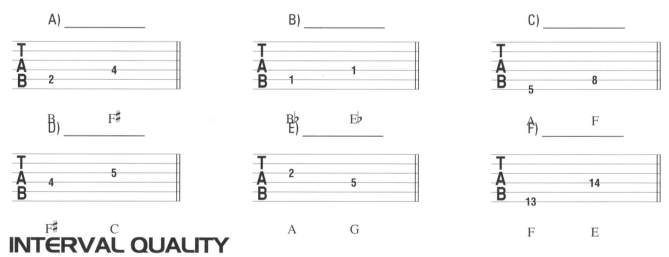

INTERVAL QUALITY

Determine the correct quantity and quality in the following pairs of notes. Again, notice whether it's going up or down. Reference the charts on page 13 and 14 if necessary. Count the note names for the quantity, and use a piano keyboard or the fretboard diagram on page 5 to count the half steps.

1. From C up to E _____

2. From G up to A♭ _____

3. From E down to C♯ _____

4. From A♯ up to B _____

5. From F up to B _____

6. From D down to G _____

Given the starting pitch, add the missing note above in tab to complete the interval.

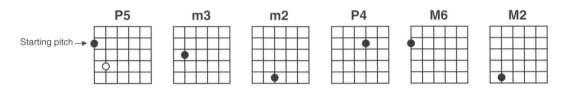

INTERVAL SHAPES

Given the starting pitch, add the appropriate note to create an interval *above*.

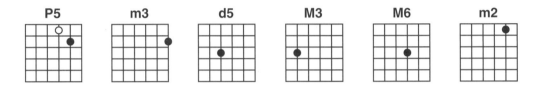

Given the starting pitch, add the appropriate note to create an interval *below* the root.

MUSICAL TERMS

Match each term in the left column with the correct description on the right.

Dot	Two notes sounded simultaneously
Augmented	Determined by counting note letter names
Interval Quality	Increases the duration of a note by 50 percent
Power Chord	A note that repeats while other notes change above or below it
Pedal Tone	One half step larger than a major or perfect interval
Harmonic Interval	Determined by counting half steps
Interval Quantity	Another name for the harmonic interval of a perfect 5th

THE MAJOR SCALE

A **scale** is a succession of notes ascending or descending in a specific order. The most common scale is the **major scale**, and it's one of the fundamental building blocks of the Western music system. But just knowing how to play one on the guitar won't do much for your understanding. We need to know how it works.

INTERVALLIC FORMULA

Every major scale—it doesn't matter what key it's in—follows the same intervallic formula of whole steps (W) and half steps (H). Here it is:

whole step – whole step – half step – whole step – whole step – whole step – half step

What this means is that, if we start on any note and follow this formula, we'll end up with a major scale built from that starting note. Let's take the note C, for example. Remembering that a half step on a guitar string is one fret and a whole step is two, let's build the C major scale. We'll work along one string for now so the intervals are easier to follow.

C MAJOR SCALE ◀30))

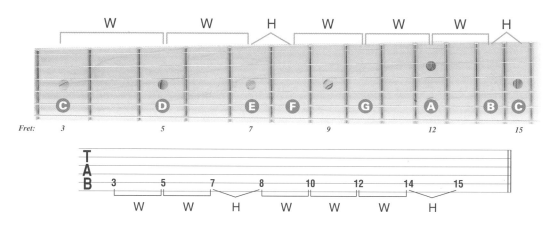

The C major scale is the only major scale that contains all natural notes, meaning no sharps or flats. All 11 other major scales contain various combinations of either sharps or flats. (A major scale only contains one or the other—sharps or flats—never both.) Let's try using the formula to build another major scale. This time, we'll use the note G:

G MAJOR SCALE ◀31))

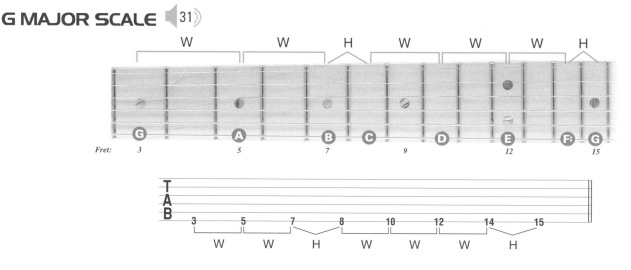

As you can see, we need one sharp (F♯) to create a G major scale. This is because the intervallic formula (W–W–H–W–W–W–H) must always remain constant in any major scale. Since the distance from E to F is only a half step, we raise F to F♯.

WHICH ENHARMONIC NAME TO USE?

You may remember that the black keys on the piano can all have two different names. In other words, the note between F and G can either be called F♯ or G♭, depending on the specific situation. So how do we know that it's called F♯ instead of G♭ in a G major scale? There are seven different letter names, and they all must appear once (and only once) in any major scale. Since we already have a G note, then the note a half step below it has to be called F♯.

Let's try building one more scale, F major, for good measure:

F MAJOR SCALE 32))

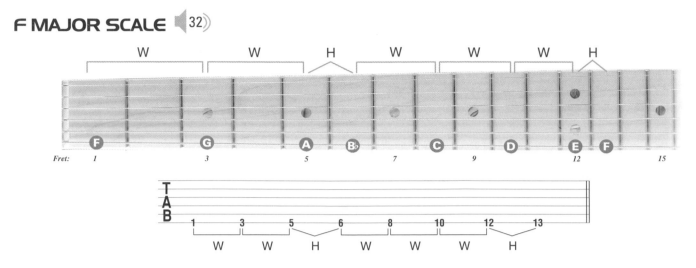

With the F major scale, we need to add a flat (B♭) to make the intervallic pattern consistent. This is because A to B is a whole step, but we need a half step in that place, so we lower B to B♭.

MAJOR SCALE PATTERNS

Of course, when we play a scale, we rarely do so on one string. Instead, we usually move some of the notes to other strings so that it's playable in one position. Let's look at a common shape for a one-octave C major scale. In this diagram, the scale's **tonic**, or **root note**, C, is shown as a square.

C MAJOR SCALE (SECOND POSITION)

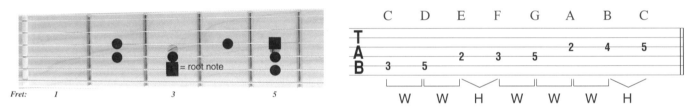

Be sure to notice that the W–W–H–W–W–W–H pattern is still in effect here. When changing strings in this pattern—from the fifth to the fourth string and from the fourth to the third string—you should recognize the intervals as a major 2nd, which is simply another name for a whole step.

Here's another common pattern for the major scale—this time in two octaves, across all six strings. This example begins with the root note, C, on the 6th string.

C MAJOR SCALE (EIGHTH POSITION)

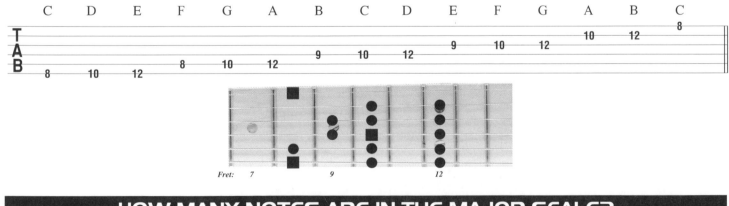

HOW MANY NOTES ARE IN THE MAJOR SCALE?

Although we typically write and play a major scale from root note to root note (C to C here), it's important to know that the scale only contains seven different notes. The "eighth" note is really just the scale starting over again in the next octave.

WHEN THE SAINTS GO MARCHING IN 🔊 33))

The notes of the major scale are the foundation for countless melodies, riffs, solos, and chord progressions. The melody to this song is based on the C major scale.

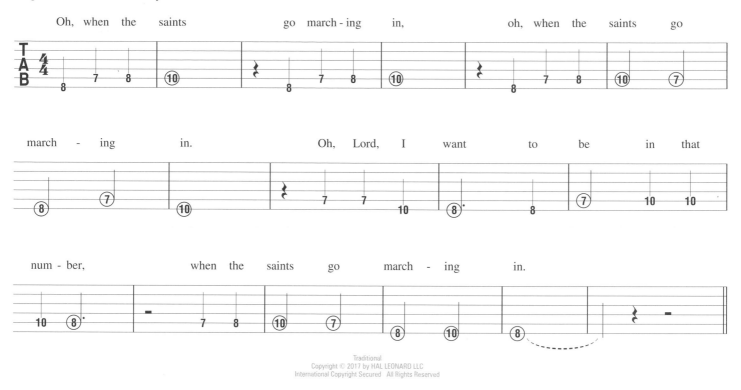

DO-RE-MI 🔊 34))

This Rodgers and Hammerstein song from *The Sound of Music* is arguably the most famous use of the major scale in popular music. The lyrics also teach the seven solfège syllables commonly used to sing the major scale. The melody uses mostly notes from the C major scale, and shifts briefly to D major and E major in measures 11 and 13, respectively.

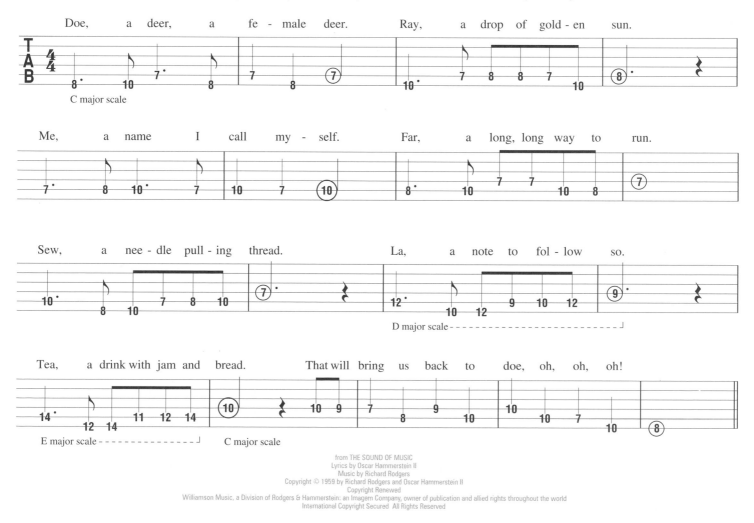

There are many patterns for playing the major scale on guitar, and it's helpful to memorize and practice them to gain knowledge of the fretboard. Here's one more essential scale pattern in two octaves that begins with the root on the 5th string.

D MAJOR SCALE

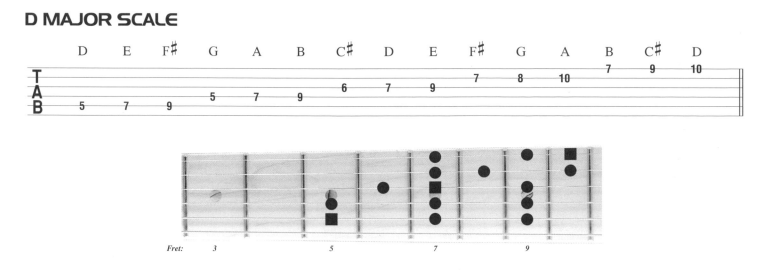

JOY TO THE WORLD 🔊35»

The first four measures of the melody to this famous Christmas carol, by Baroque composer George Frideric Handel, comes right down the D major scale.

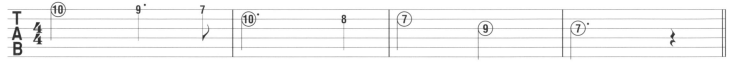

MAJOR SCALE CHART

Major scales are the building blocks of music, and music theory. Chords and chord progressions are also derived from scales. Following is a handy table that spells the notes in all 12 keys. Don't get bogged down trying to memorize all this at once, but you might want to dog-ear this page for future reference.

	1 (root)	2	3	4	5	6	7
C major	C	D	E	F	G	A	B
G major	G	A	B	C	D	E	F#
D major	D	E	F#	G	A	B	C#
A major	A	B	C#	D	E	F#	G#
E major	E	F#	G#	A	B	C#	D#
B major	B	C#	D#	E	F#	G#	A#
F# major	F#	G#	A#	B	C#	D#	E#
Db major	Db	Eb	F	Gb	Ab	Bb	C
Ab major	Ab	Bb	C	Db	Eb	F	G
Eb major	Eb	F	G	Ab	Bb	C	D
Bb major	Bb	C	D	Eb	F	G	A
F major	F	G	A	Bb	C	D	E

CHORDS: PART 1

A **chord** is a collection of three or more notes arranged (usually) in a harmonious fashion. You may already know how to play hundreds of chords, but this section deals with how they're constructed and why they sound the way they do.

TRIADS

This is the most common type of chord in all of pop and rock music. The **triad** is a chord that contains three different notes—hence the name. Traditionally, there are four types of triads: major, minor, augmented, and diminished. Each one contains a root (the note after which the chord is named), a 3rd (which is a 3rd interval above the root), and a 5th (a 5th interval above the root). Each triad has a formula:

- **Major triad**: root, major 3rd, perfect 5th
- **Minor triad**: root, minor 3rd, perfect 5th
- **Augmented triad**: root, major 3rd, augmented 5th
- **Diminished triad**: root, minor 3rd, diminished 5th

When found within a piece of music, these four triads are commonly notated with chord symbols like this:

	C Major	C Minor	C Augmented	C Diminished
Chord symbol:	**C**	**Cm**, or **Cmin**	**C+**, or **Caug**	**C°**, or **Cdim**

Here are the different kinds of triads built from the root note C on the 6th string, 8th fret. When you play them, notice the kind of sound that each evokes. Major chords have a cheerful sound while minor chords perhaps sound more melancholy. The other two are a little more difficult to describe, but some say an augmented chord sounds like a question waiting anxiously to be answered, while a diminished chord sounds dark and mysterious.

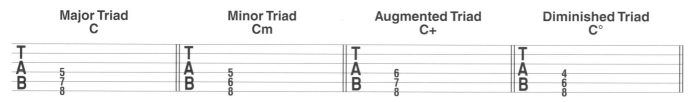

CALYPSO 🔊 36))

When the individual notes of a triad or chord are picked in succession, it's called an arpeggio. Here's a riff that uses major triads in three different positions (D, G, and A chords). The rhythms are a little tricky, so listen to the audio track for reference.

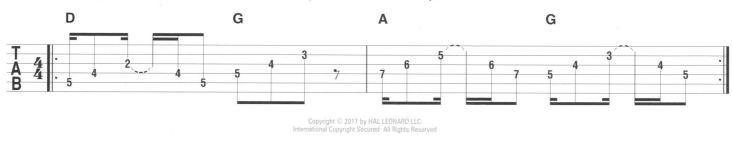

MINOR MOOD 🔊 37))

Here's a chord progression that uses only minor triads.

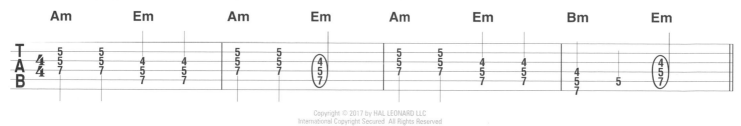

Major and minor chords are by far the most commonly used throughout all styles of music, while augmented and diminished are found less frequently. That's because augmented and diminished chords have a dissonant quality, or harshness, to their sound. Normally, these types of chords are used to create musical tension which is resolved by moving to a major or minor chord.

IN TENSION 38

Here's a progression that incorporates an A augmented (A+) triad. The chords in this example have four notes instead of three because the root notes are doubled.

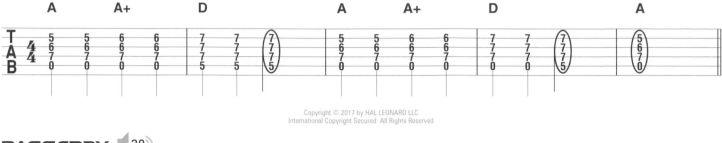

PASSERBY 39

In this example, the diminished chords are used to pass smoothly between the major and minor triads.

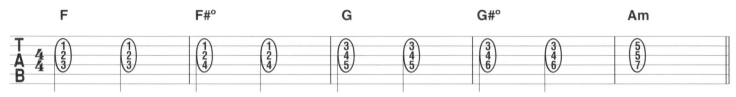

To hear an example of an augmented chord in popular music, check out the very first chord played in the Beatles song "Oh! Darling," or the first chord in Chuck Berry's "School Days." For diminished, listen for the 2nd chord played in the verses of Garth Brooks' song "Friends in Low Places."

CHORD VOICINGS

If you've played guitar for any amount of time, you'll know that the major and minor triad shapes in the previous section don't look much like the chord shapes we're used to playing. That's because in most of our normal chord shapes, or **voicings**, notes of the triad have been rearranged and doubled in different octaves to produce fuller-sounding and easier-to-play chords.

Let's examine the common, open C chord as an example:

We can see that it contains two C notes (root), two E notes (major 3rd), and one G note (perfect 5th) for a total of five notes. But it's still only three *different* notes: C, E, and G.

Let's look at an open G chord:

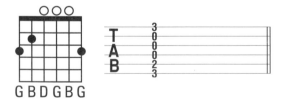

This chord contains three G notes (root), two B notes (major 3rd), and one D note (perfect 5th) for a total of six notes. But it's still a three-note major triad.

And here's an open A minor chord:

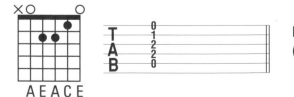

Here we have two A notes (root), one C note (minor 3rd), and two E notes (perfect 5th) for a total of five notes. It's still a three-note minor triad.

HARMONIZING THE MAJOR SCALE

When we harmonize the major scale, we build a chord off of each of its notes. We typically assign either numbers and/or Roman numerals to the degrees (notes) of the scale to help more quickly identify them and to aid in transposition, which we'll discuss later.

For example, we'll assign numbers to the notes of the C major scale as follows:

C	D	E	F	G	A	B
1	2	3	4	5	6	7
I	ii	iii	IV	V	vi	vii°

(Read on to find out why some Roman numerals are uppercase and some lowercase.)

To harmonize the scale, we're going to build a chord off each of these notes, using a process called **stacking 3rds**. To stack 3rds, add two notes to each scale degree in an every-other-note manner. This will result in a root, 3rd, and 5th for each scale degree. (The chord's 3rd is a 3rd interval above the root, and the chord's 5th is a 3rd interval above the chord's 3rd—hence the term "stacking 3rds.")

For example, if we want to build a chord from the first note of the C major scale, which is C, we'd do the following:

- Start with C, the root
- Go to the 3rd note of the scale, E, skipping a note (D)
- Go to the 5th note of the scale, G, skipping a note (F)

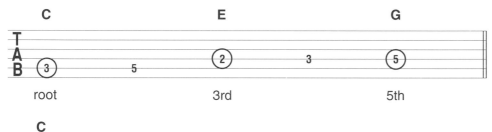

A C major chord is spelled C–E–G. Of course, since we want to play this as a chord, we'll need to move the G note over a string, so we'll place it at the open third string.

How do we know that this is a C major triad? Well, look at the intervals: from C to E is a major 3rd, and from C to G is a perfect 5th.

Let's try one more. If we want to build a triad from the second note of the C major scale, D, we'd do this:

- Start with D
- Add the note two degrees up from D in the scale (F)
- Add the note two degrees up from F in the scale (A)

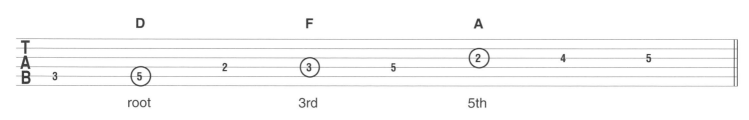

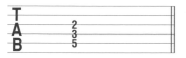

By doing this, we end up with a D minor triad. D up to F is a minor 3rd interval, and D to A is a perfect 5th.

If we repeat this process for each note in the C major scale, we'll get the following:

HARMONIZED C MAJOR SCALE 40

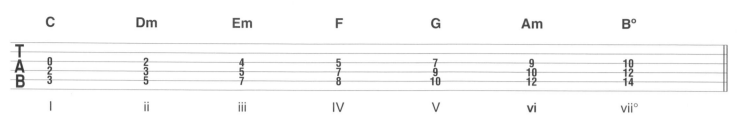

C	Dm	Em	F	G	Am	B°
I	ii	iii	IV	V	vi	vii°

There are three different types of chords in this harmonized major scale (see symbols above the staff): major, minor, and diminished.

- As noted earlier, a letter-name-only chord symbol is understood to mean a major triad. So, in the above figure, there are three major triads: C, F, and G.

- The "m" in a chord symbol indicates a minor triad. So, there are three minor triads above: Dm, Em, and Am.

- The "°" in a chord symbol indicates a diminished triad. There's only one diminished triad above: B°. (You'll occasionally see "dim" used instead of the ° symbol.)

Notice that the uppercase Roman numerals correspond to the major chords, and the lowercase ones correspond to the minor chords. And vii° is used for the diminished chord.

What About the Augmented Triad?

You may have noticed that the augmented triad is not present in the harmonized C major scale. This is correct. In fact, you won't see an augmented triad in any major scale; they only appear in specific musical situations that are a bit more sophisticated.

THE HARMONIZED MAJOR SCALE FORMULA

The order of major, minor, and diminished triads in the harmonized C major scale above actually represents another useful formula, similar to the W–W–H–W–W–W–H one used to build a major scale. Every major scale contains the same order of **diatonic** triads—diatonic simply means "of the key"—when harmonized:

Major	Minor	Minor	Major	Major	Minor	Diminished
I	ii	iii	IV	V	vi	vii°

So, if we want to know the diatonic chords in the key of G major, for example, we simply substitute the notes of that scale and apply the chord formula.

HARMONIZED G MAJOR SCALE 41

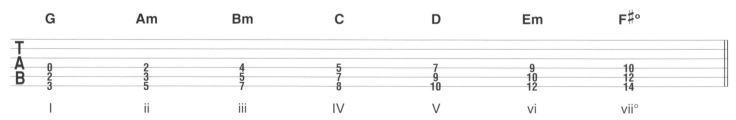

G	Am	Bm	C	D	Em	F#°
I	ii	iii	IV	V	vi	vii°

CHECKPOINT 3

TRIADS

1. How many notes are in a triad? _____

2. How many types of triads are there? _____

3. What are their names? _____

Identify the following triads by their formula:

4. Root, major 3rd, augmented 5th: _____

5. Root, minor 3rd, perfect 5th: _____

6. Root, minor 3rd, diminished 5th: _____

7. Root, major 3rd, perfect 5th: _____

Identify the following triads by the tab notation. (**Hint:** Not all of them fall within the C major or G major scale. Identify the root and then use the triad formulas to figure out any that you don't know.)

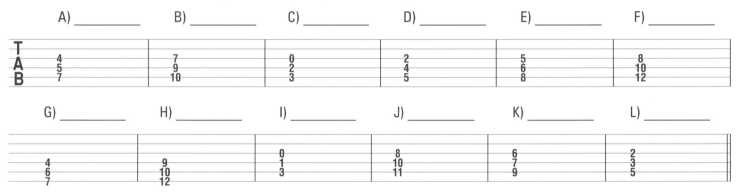

A) _____   B) _____   C) _____   D) _____   E) _____   F) _____

G) _____   H) _____   I) _____   J) _____   K) _____   L) _____

HARMONIZED MAJOR SCALE

1. What do uppercase Roman numerals indicate? _____ Lowercase ones? _____

2. How many minor triads exist within any major scale? _____

3. How many diminished triads exist within any major scale? _____

4. What is the harmonized major scale triad formula in Roman numerals? _____

Given the key, and knowing the harmonized major scale formula, fill in the missing chords:

5. Key of C major: C, Dm, Em, F, G, _____, B°

6. Key of G major: G, Am, Bm, C, _____, Em, F#°

7. Key of B♭ major: B♭, Cm, _____, E♭, F, Gm, A°

MUSICAL TERMS

Match each term in the left column with the correct description on the right.

Stacking 3rds	A note or chord belonging to the key
Diatonic	A chord containing three different notes
Root	Building chords with a scale, using the every-other-note process
Triad	A note or chord that doesn't belong to the key
Non-diatonic	The note after which a chord is named

CHORDS: Part 2

Now that you have a bit of chord knowledge under your belt, let's look at how they're used.

TRANSPOSING CHORD PROGRESSIONS

A **chord progression** is simply the order in which chords progress in a song. The beauty of the Roman numeral system is that chord progressions can easily be transposed from key to key. For example, let's take a look at a common chord progression in the key of G: G to C.

42)) **Key of G: G–C**

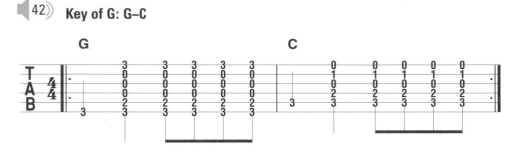

In order to transpose this chord progression to another key, we simply follow these steps:

1. Write out the notes of the major scale matching the key: In this case, that's the G major scale.
2. Beneath the notes, write the harmonized major scale formula.
3. Treating each note as a chord symbol, match each to its corresponding Roman numeral—i.e., major = letter name only, minor = added "m," etc.

G	Am	Bm	C	D	Em	F#°
I	ii	iii	IV	V	vi	vii°

As we can see, G is the I chord, and C is the IV chord. So a G–C progression in the key of G can also be called a I–IV progression.

Let's say we want to transpose this to the key of C major. We just write out the C major scale, add the harmonized major scale formula beneath it, and adjust the chord symbols.

C	Dm	Em	F	G	Am	B°
I	ii	iii	IV	V	vi	vii°

And there you have it: a I–IV progression in the key of C is C–F.

43)) **Key of C: C–F**

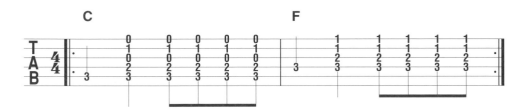

Here's another common progression, arranged here in the key of D.

44)) Key of D: D–A–Bm–G

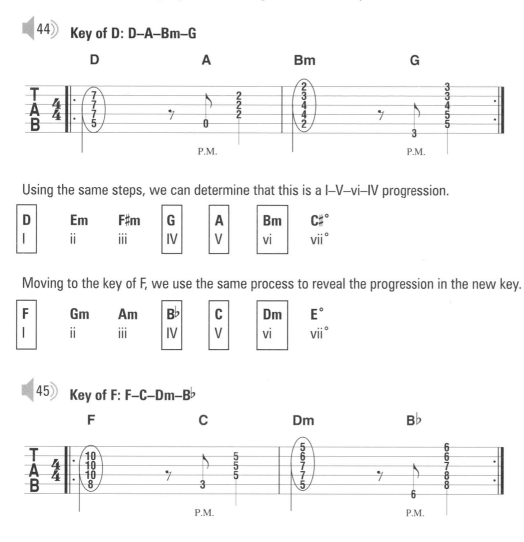

Using the same steps, we can determine that this is a I–V–vi–IV progression.

D	Em	F#m	G	A	Bm	C#°
I	ii	iii	IV	V	vi	vii°

Moving to the key of F, we use the same process to reveal the progression in the new key.

F	Gm	Am	B♭	C	Dm	E°
I	ii	iii	IV	V	vi	vii°

45)) Key of F: F–C–Dm–B♭

Another common progression is I–IV–V–IV. If we wanted to play this progression in the key of A major, we simply follow the steps outlined previously.

A	Bm	C#m	D	E	F#m	G#°
I	ii	iii	IV	V	vi	vii°

So the I chord is A, the IV chord is D, and the V chord is E.

46)) Key of A: A–D–E–D

Let's check out some songs that make use of these progressions.

There are probably hundreds of songs to choose from when it comes to the I–IV–V progression and variations of it. Whitesnake made use of it for the chorus of their '80s rock anthem "Here I Go Again," played in the key of G. Note that, even though these chords are voiced as power chords, their major tonality is implied by the vocal melody.

Key of G

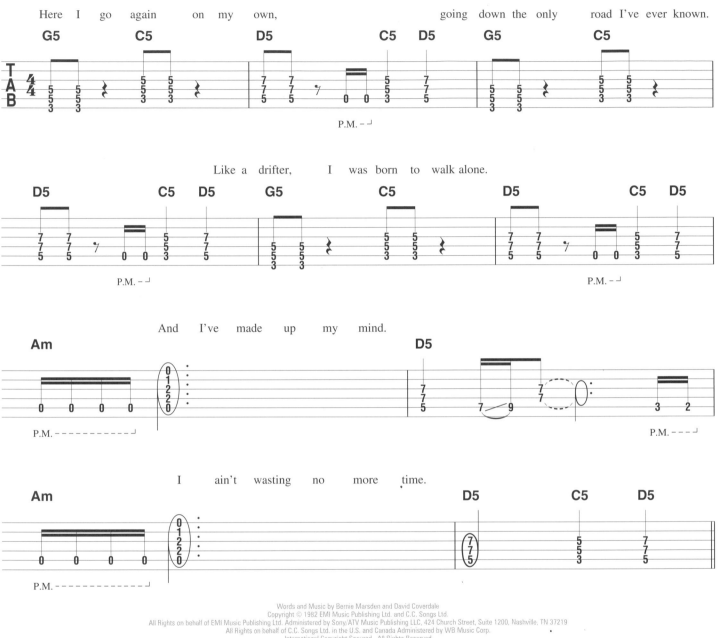

POWER CHORDS

Power chords are popular in certain styles of music like rock and metal because of their heavy, low sound. They are normally played on the lower strings (with the root note on either the 5th or 6th string), and contain only the root note and the 5th above the root—no 3rd. The three-note version of the chord doubles the root above the 5th, but is not considered a triad because it still contains only two *different* notes. The symbol for these chords shows the root name with the number 5 beside it, for instance, G5, C5, and D5.

I STILL HAVEN'T FOUND WHAT I'M LOOKING FOR 🔊 48))

The chords within a progression can last longer than only a few beats as demonstrated with U2's "I Still Haven't Found What I'm Looking For." Presented here in the key of A, the verses make use of a I–IV progression, but with the I chord dominating throughout. (Don't miss the variation of the I–IV–V progression that appears in the chorus as V–IV–I.) At the end of the chorus, there are **numbered endings**: Play from the beginning of the chorus (the open repeat sign) to the closing repeat sign under the first bracket and then go back to the beginning of the chorus. On the second time through, skip over the first ending and go directly to the second bracketed ending.

Key of A

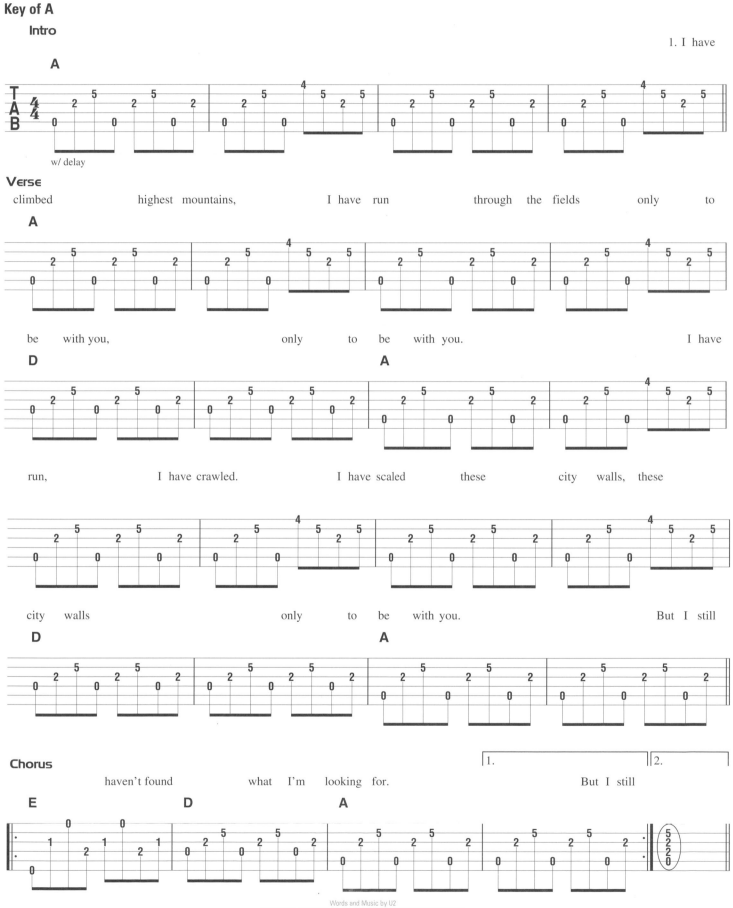

NO WOMAN NO CRY 49

The I–V–vi–IV progression has had plenty of use in popular music throughout the years. Some examples include Green Day's "When I Come Around," Jason Mraz's "I'm Yours," and "Beast of Burden" by the Rolling Stones. In Bob Marley's classic song, "No Woman No Cry," it is used throughout the verse section. In the intro and chorus sections, the progression is extended to become I–V–vi–IV, followed by I–IV–I–V.

Key of C

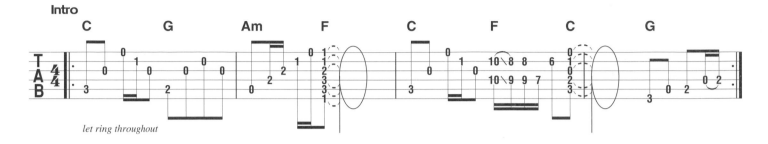

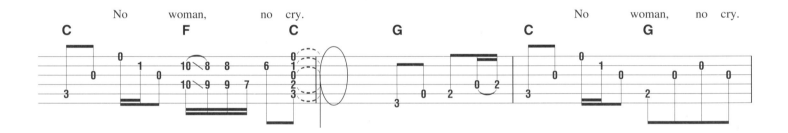

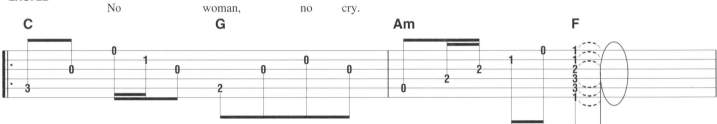

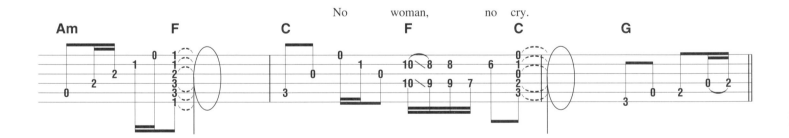

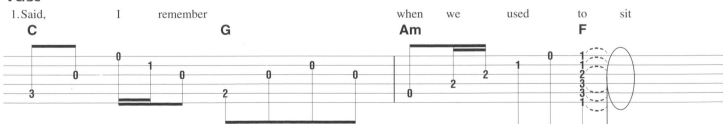

in the government yard in Trench Town.

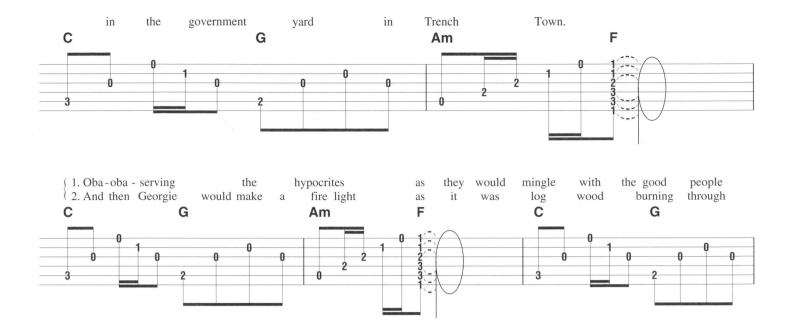

1. Oba - oba - serving the hypocrites as they would mingle with the good people
2. And then Georgie would make a fire light as it was log wood burning through

we meet.
the night.

Goodfriends we had, oh, good friends we lost
Then we would cook cornmeal porridge

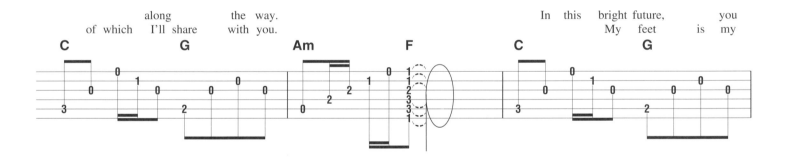

along the way.
of which I'll share with you.

In this bright future, you
My feet is my

can't forget your past, so dry your tears I say.
only carriage so I've got to push on through, but while I'm gone...

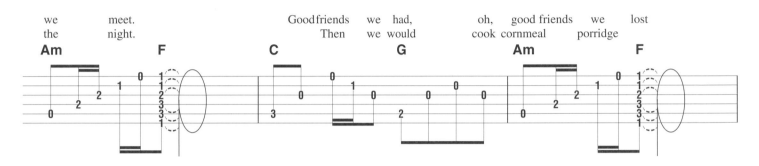

Repeat & fade

Everything's gonna be all right. Everything's gonna be all right.

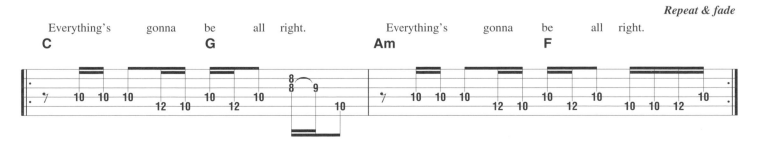

ALL I HAVE TO DO IS DREAM 🔊 50)

The I–vi–IV–V progression was a widely-used vehicle for pop songs in the fifties like this one made famous by the Everly Brothers. Other songs featuring this progression include Ben E. King's "Stand by Me," "Happiness Is a Warm Gun" by The Beatles, and "D'yer Mak'er" by Led Zeppelin.

Key of E

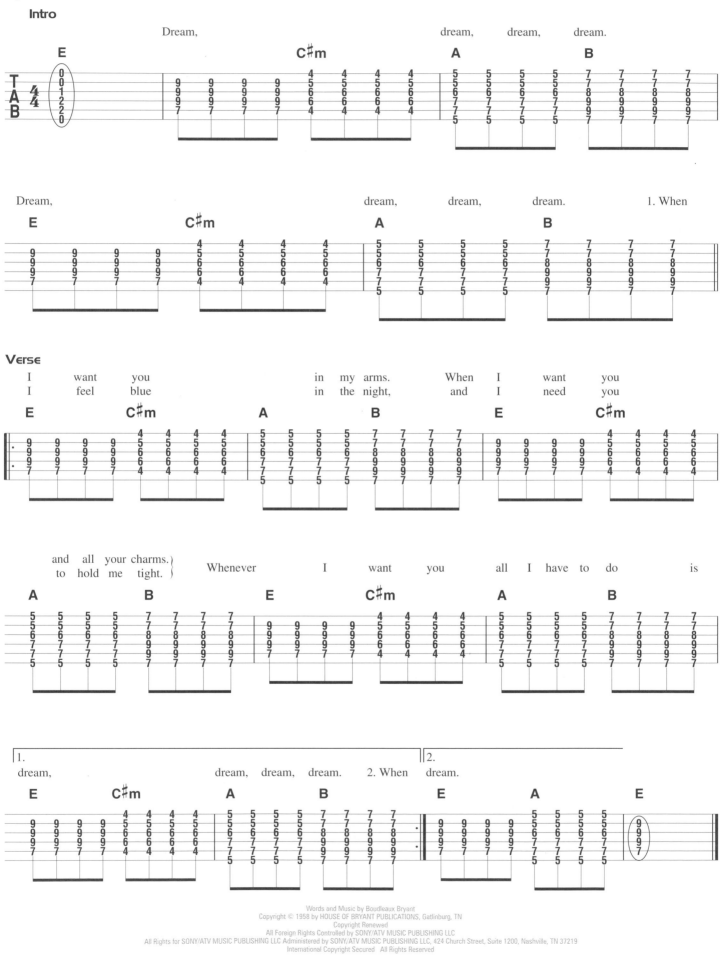

Words and Music by Boudleaux Bryant
Copyright © 1958 by HOUSE OF BRYANT PUBLICATIONS, Gatlinburg, TN
Copyright Renewed
All Foreign Rights Controlled by SONY/ATV MUSIC PUBLISHING LLC
All Rights for SONY/ATV MUSIC PUBLISHING LLC Administered by SONY/ATV MUSIC PUBLISHING LLC, 424 Church Street, Suite 1200, Nashville, TN 37219
International Copyright Secured All Rights Reserved

THE MINOR SCALE

You already know the intervallic formula for the major scale (W–W–H–W–W–W–H), and by this point should be able to construct a major scale in any key. Using this knowledge as a base, you can learn to build other types of scales, such as the minor scale, but with a different approach.

THE NUMERIC FORMULA

To build the minor scale (also known as **natural minor** to differentiate from other minor scales), let's first assign a number to each note in the major scale. Here's the C major scale:

C	D	E	F	G	A	B
1	2	3	4	5	6	7

Next, we'll apply the **numeric formula** for the natural minor scale, which is 1–2–♭3–4–5–♭6–♭7. This means we have to lower the third, sixth, and seventh degrees of the C major scale to get a C minor scale:

C	D	E♭	F	G	A♭	B♭
1	2	♭3	4	5	♭6	♭7

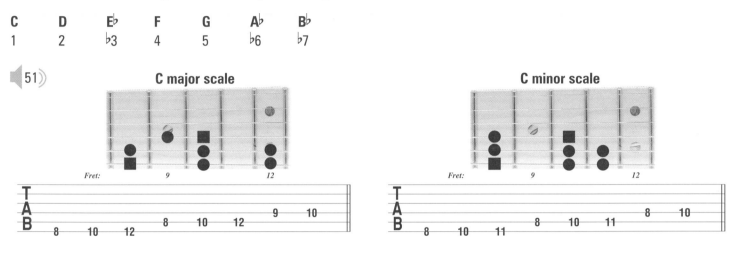

Let's try the same thing beginning with the G major scale:

G	A	B	C	D	E	F♯
1	2	3	4	5	6	7

Note that the flats in the numerical formula simply tell you to lower the note by one half step. Therefore, in the case of the G minor scale, we add flats to B and E, but F♯ simply becomes F. Think of it as akin to the relationship between major and minor intervals. A "7" in a major scale formula represents a major 7th (M7), whereas a "♭7" represents a minor 7th (m7).

G	A	B♭	C	D	E♭	F
1	2	♭3	4	5	♭6	♭7

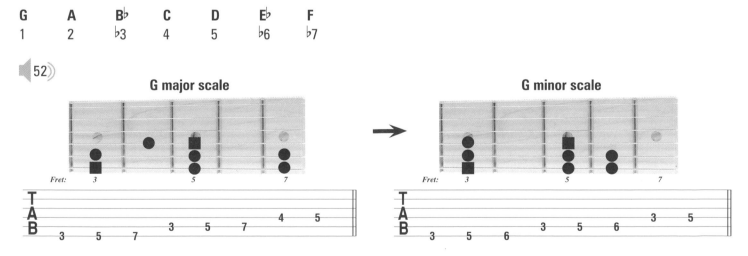

There is an intervallic formula for the natural minor scale as well: W–H–W–W–H–W–W. However, I think you'll find the numeric formula much more effective than having to learn a new intervallic formula for every new scale you learn in the future.

If we play a minor scale built from a root note on the 5th string, the one-octave fretboard pattern remains the same. Here is the scale beginning with the root note (D) on the 5th fret of the 5th string.

D minor scale

GOD REST YE MERRY, GENTLEMEN 🔊 53»

The melody of this traditional Christmas carol is built from the minor scale. The scale pattern here begins with the root note (D) on the 5th string.

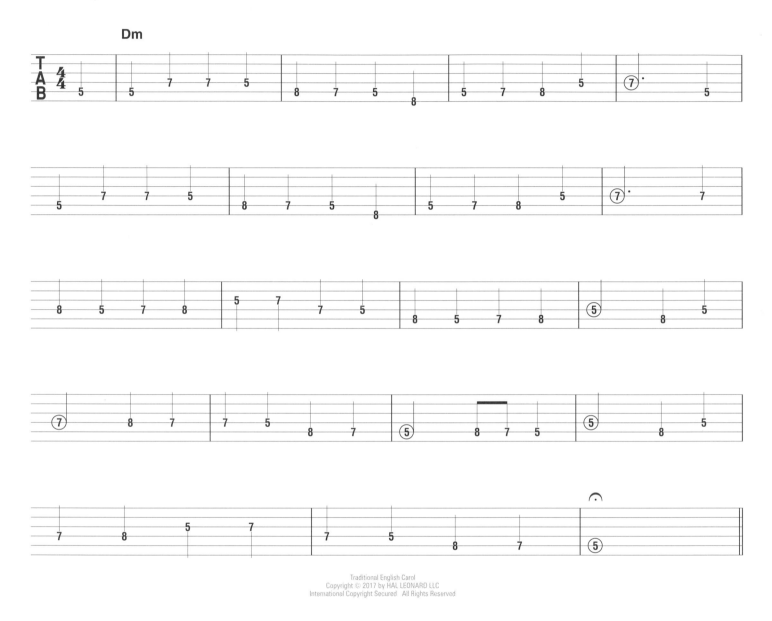

BLACK SUNDAY ROCK 🔊 54»

The A minor scale sets the dark mood for this hard rock riff.

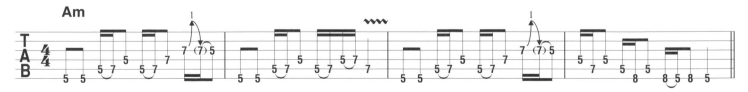

ESSENTIAL MINOR SCALE PATTERNS

Learning the entire guitar fretboard and being able to find the notes of a scale in any position on the neck is a daunting task that can take years of practice. But whether you're a casual player, or are on the road to becoming a professional, there are a couple essential minor scale patterns everyone should memorize first.

These scale patterns span two octaves each, the first with the root note on the 6th string, and the second with the root on the 5th string. Both patterns are movable, meaning that no matter which root note you choose as your starting point, the pattern of notes on the fretboard stays the same.

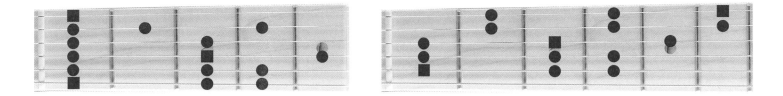

HARMONIZING THE MINOR SCALE

Just like we did with the major scale earlier in the book on page 27, the minor scale can be harmonized to create a series of triads (chords) by stacking 3rds. We'll use Roman numerals again to label the chords, but this time they'll follow the numeric formula of the minor scale. Let's look at the A minor scale to start.

A MINOR SCALE

A	B	C	D	E	F	G
1	2	♭3	4	5	♭6	♭7

HARMONIZED A MINOR SCALE 🔊 55))

Am	B°	C	Dm	Em	F	G
i	ii°	♭III	iv	v	♭VI	♭VII

Instead of literally stacking 3rds as we did before with the major scale, we're going to assume you understand the concept and show this harmonized minor scale with normal guitar voicings.

Am	B°	C	Dm	Em	F	G
i	ii°	♭III	iv	v	♭VI	♭VII

```
T   0           3           5           7           8           10
A   1       3   5       6   8       9   10      10  12
    2       4   5       7   9       9   10      10  12
B   2       3   5       7   9       9   10      10  12
    0       2   3       5   7       7   8       8   10
```

Let's try the same thing beginning on E. The second degree of the E minor scale is F# because of the whole step up from the root.

HARMONIZED E MINOR SCALE 🔊 56))

Em	F#°	G	Am	Bm	C	D
i	ii°	♭III	iv	v	♭VI	♭VII

Em	F#°	G	Am	Bm	C	D
i	ii°	♭III	iv	v	♭VI	♭VII

```
T   0               3           5           7           8           10
A   0           2   3       2   5       7   7       10  8       10  10
    0           4   4       2   5       7   9       10  9       11
B   2           3   5       5   7       9   10      10  12
    2               5           7           7           10          12
    0           2   3       2   5       7   7       8       10
```

MINOR CHORD PROGRESSIONS

Earlier, we looked at common chord progressions and songs in major keys, but as you may know, music can also be in a minor key. This just means that the tonic chord in piece of music—the one that sounds like "home base"—is a minor chord. Some popular rock songs in a minor key are "Refugee" by Tom Petty, "House of the Rising Sun" by the Animals, and "Stairway to Heaven" by Led Zeppelin. Here are a few examples of typical minor-key progressions.

THE MINOR CLIMB 57

The ♭VI–♭VII–i progression, and many variations of it, is extremely common in rock and pop. Here's an example in one of the most common keys for it, A minor.

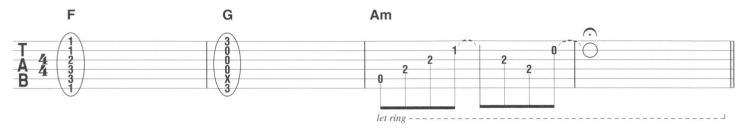

MINOR BLUES 58

There are many different forms of the minor blues (just as there are with standard blues), but one common form uses the diatonic i, iv, and v chords. Here's an example in the key of E minor:

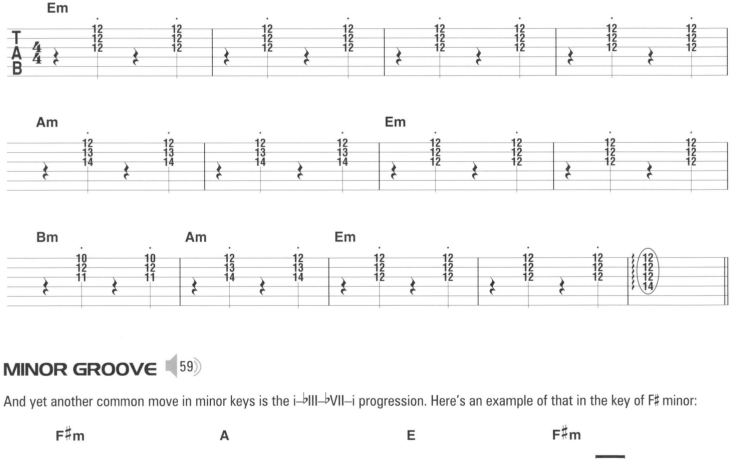

MINOR GROOVE 59

And yet another common move in minor keys is the i–♭III–♭VII–i progression. Here's an example of that in the key of F♯ minor:

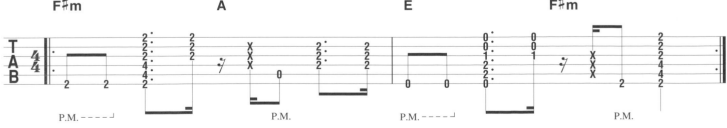

THE V–I CADENCE

Arguably the most important of all the diatonic chords in either the minor or major scales are the **tonic** and **dominant**. The tonic is another name for the 1st scale degree (root note), or chord built from the 1st degree. Dominant is another name for the 5th scale degree, or the chord built from that degree.

Why are they so important? It's because they are the most common ingredients of a typical **harmonic cadence**—a progression leading to the resolution, or end, of a section or song. A cadence tells the listener what key the piece of music is in because it leads to the tonic of the key. Cadences of many different types are found all throughout Western classical and popular music, and of them all, the most common is V–I.

Here's an example of a V–I cadence, also called an authentic cadence, in the key of A that could end a rock song. Cadences can be subtler than this one, but here the V chord (E) is held a few measures for a climactic ending.

THE BIG ENDING 🔊 60))

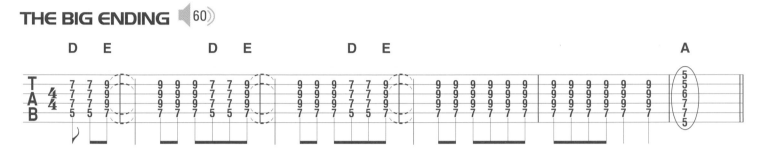

One reason the V–I cadence is used so much is that the V chord (in a major key) contains the leading tone of the tonic. The **leading tone** is the note one half step below the root of the tonic chord, and sonically speaking, wants to pull to the tonic to resolve. That leading-tone-to-tonic resolution has a pleasing sound that has been used in music for hundreds of years!

In the V chord, the 3rd is the leading tone of the key. For example, in the key of A, the 3rd of the V chord is G♯. That note is one half step below the root of the tonic chord (A). In the key of C, the 3rd of the V chord is B. That leading tone resolves up to C.

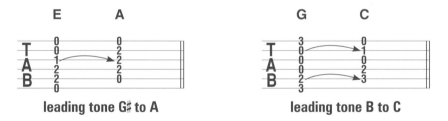

leading tone G♯ to A   leading tone B to C

There can be nearly any combination of chords preceding the V–I cadence, but simply moving from a V to a I chord does not make a cadence. The other factor necessary is that the feeling of landing on the I chord has some sense of finality or arrival.

For another example of this cadence, listen to the song "Last Kiss"—a fifties song covered by Pearl Jam—with each verse and chorus ending on the tonic, G major. The whole song is a repeating I–vi–IV–V progression (G–Em–C–D), but at the end of each verse and chorus they land on G and hold it for two measures. This cadential pause sets up the next verse or chorus section.

FUNCTIONAL NAMES

The harmonized chords or scale degrees of the major scale go by another set of names, as well, based on their typical functions:

I = Tonic: Tonal center

ii = Supertonic: Directly above the Tonic

iii = Mediant: Halfway between the Tonic and Dominant

IV = Subdominant: Directly below the Dominant

V = Dominant: Second most common (after the Tonic)

vi = Submediant: Halfway between the Tonic and Subdominant

vii° = Leading Tone: A half step below the Tonic, to which it leads with strong resolution

THE MINOR DOMINANT CHORD

You may remember that when harmonizing the natural minor scale by stacking thirds, the triad based on the 5th degree is minor in quality. This is diatonically correct, but doesn't make for a very strong resolution when moving from dominant to tonic because the leading tone is not present.

Listen to the following progression in the key of A minor:

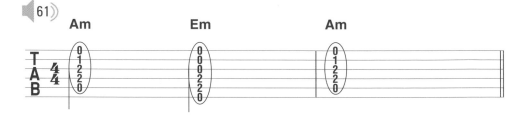

Notice that the Em chord has a G note, whereas the leading tone (a half step below the tonic) would be G#. This is not present in the natural minor scale. Therefore, oftentimes the major V chord will be substituted to create a stronger resolution. Listen to the progression now:

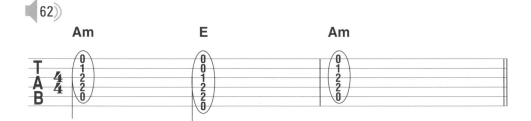

It sounds much more resolved, don't you think?

THE MINOR DESCENT 63

Here's a chord progression in B minor (I–♭VII–♭VI–V) that includes the major dominant V chord. This progression is the basis of songs like "Walk Don't Run" by the Ventures and "Stray Cat Strut" by the Stray Cats, plus many others.

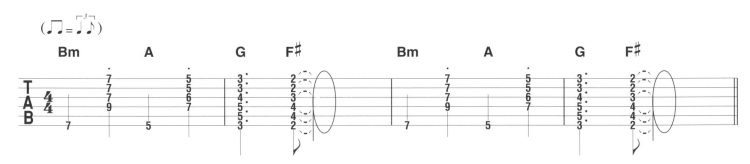

BEYOND TRIADS

Triads are the backbone of all modern popular and rock music harmony, but guitarists and songwriters often venture beyond standard, three-note chords to create more sonic "color." To make more interesting sounding chords, guitarists can add notes on top of triads. These additions can be taken from major and minor scales, or even intervals that lie outside of those scales.

THE NUMERIC CODE

If you've looked at much guitar sheet music, you may have seen some interesting-looking chord symbols that contain numbers, like Amaj7, Dm7, G6, or Cadd9. These additions to the chord root names give us information on what notes are attached to a triad.

To find out which notes are in these chords, break them into two parts: First, decipher whether the basic triad is major or minor. (We'll exclude diminished and augmented triads from this section to focus on chords that are more commonly found.) As you remember, major triads are named using the root letter only—i.e. A, C, and F. Minor triads contain a small "m" beside the root name. Therefore, a chord called Gm6 is built on the notes of a G-minor triad, while G6 is built on a G-major triad.

The second part to these chords is the number that follows the triad name. This number corresponds to a note at an interval above the root. In other words, a G6 chord is built from a G major triad with an added 6th above the root (E).

AMERICANA 🔊64))

Here's a short example to demonstrate how one common voicing of the G6 chord sounds. Whichever finger you use to play the G on the 6th string must also touch the 5th string to mute it.

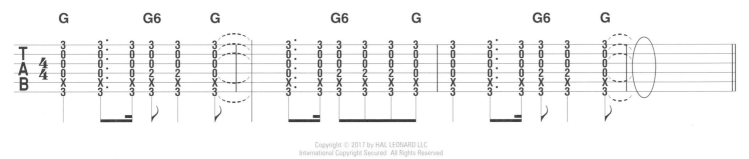

DARK ARPEGGIO 🔊65))

Likewise, a Gm6 chord is built from a G-minor triad with an added 6th (E again). It has a dark sound due to the minor quality of the triad. The 6th in this chord voicing is found both on the 1st and 4th strings.

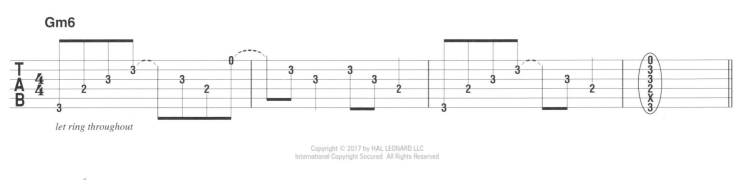

let ring throughout

SPIES 🔊66))

Another type of 6th chord is the minor flat-6 (m♭6). This one has a minor 6th above the root of the triad, and its most notable use is in the classic spy theme chord progression.

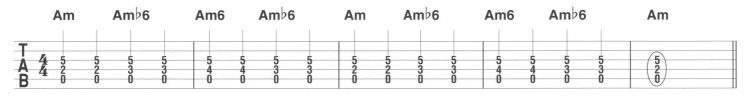

SEVENTH CHORDS

The simplest way of describing a seventh chord such as Dm7, D7, or Dmaj7, is to say that these chords contain a note a 7th above their root. An important thing to remember about seventh chords, is that a plain "7" means a minor 7th interval above the root, while maj7 means a note a major 7th interval above the root.

DOMINANT SEVEN 67))

The seventh chord built on a major triad with a minor 7th on top—also known as a **dominant seventh chord**—is especially common in blues and jazz music, but is found in rock and many other styles as well. Here's a C7–F7 chord progression played in a funky rhythm called the Bo Diddley Beat. The B♭ on the 3rd string is the 7th of C and E♭ is the 7th of F.

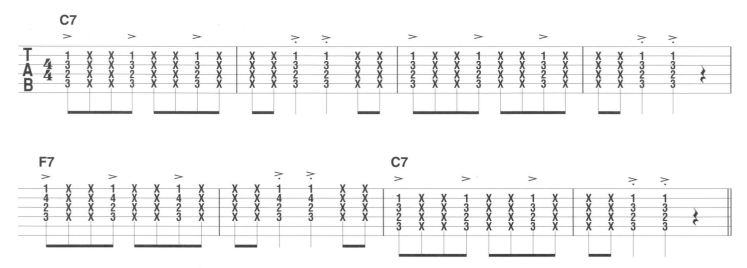

MAJOR SEVEN 68))

The **major seventh chord** is also built on a major triad, but with a major 7th interval added above the chord root. The major 7th above F is E, and the major 7th above C is B.

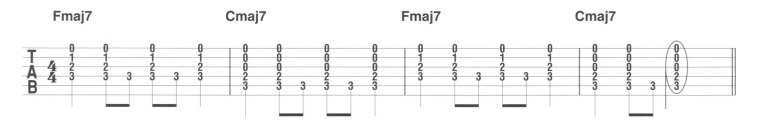

MINOR SEVEN 69))

When we add a minor 7th to a minor triad we get a regular **minor seventh chord**. If the interval added to the triad is a major 7th, it becomes a **minor-major seventh chord**. Here's a chord progression that begins with a D minor triad, then moves between the two types of minor seventh chords.

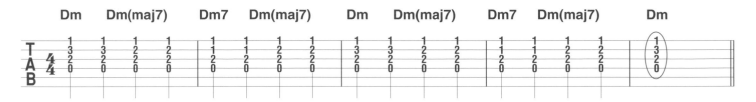

SUSPENDED CHORDS

A **suspended** (or sus) chord is a chord that lacks a 3rd. The omitted major or minor 3rd of a normal triad is replaced by either a perfect 4th or a major 2nd. Therefore, a **sus4** chord is comprised of a root, 4th, and 5th, and a **sus2** chord contains a root, 2nd, and 5th. The sound of these chords can be described as somewhat unstable, as the suspended note wants to pull, or resolve, to the 3rd.

FREE WHEELIN' 70

Suspended chords can be heard in many well-known rock and pop songs like Michael Jackson's "Black or White," and in the main chord progression of Tom Petty's "Free Fallin'." In these songs, the suspended notes resolve to the major 3rd, as they do in the following example.

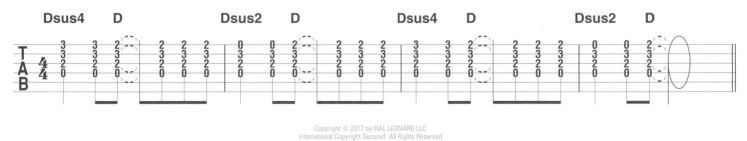

MINOR SUS 71

Here's what same sus chords sound like when resolving to a minor 3rd.

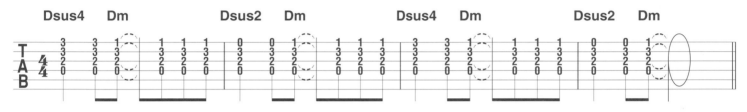

ADD 2 72

It is also possible to combine the notes of a triad—including its 3rd—with a major 2nd, resulting in an **add2 chord**. The resulting sound is more stable than a sus chord since the 3rd is included, so the addition of a 2nd simply contributes sonic color to a triad.

Cadd2   C   Cmaj7   Cadd2   Asus4   Am   Asus2   Asus4   Cadd2

MINOR ADD 2 73

For contrast, here's a progression that demonstrates the difference in sound between major and minor add2 chords. To play the A chord, barre across strings 2 through 4 on the 2nd fret using your first finger, and use your third finger for the B note on string 3.

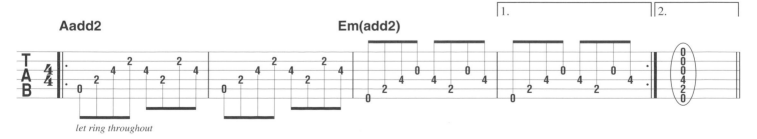

let ring throughout

There are many more chords that can be created using various combinations of triads and notes; the examples given in this book are just the tip of the iceberg. Feel free to experiment with your own combinations and see what interesting chord creations you can make!

APPENDIX

CHECKPOINT 1 ANSWER KEY

NOTE NAMES

A) F

B) D

C) C# or D♭

D) A# or B♭

MUSICAL TERMS

Staccato = Short and clipped

Tie = A curved, dashed line joining the rhythmic values of two notes

Shuffle feel = An indication to play eighth notes in a lopsided manner

Enharmonic = One note having two different names

Interval = The musical distance between notes

Octave = The distance between one note and another higher or lower note with the same name

Bar line = Divides the music on the staff into measures

INTERVALS AND THE MUSICAL ALPHABET

Which letters are used in the musical alphabet? A, B, C, D, E, F, and G

How many frets equal one half step on the guitar? One fret

How many frets equal one whole step on the guitar? Two frets

Where do the natural half steps occur in the musical alphabet? Between E and F, and also between B and C

What is the enharmonic name for the note A#? B♭

A) half step

B) whole step

C) half step

D) A to B♭: half step

E) D to E: whole step

F) B to C#: whole step

G) F to G♭: half step

CHECKPOINT 2 ANSWER KEY

INTERVAL QUANTITY

1. 4th
2. 2nd
3. 6th
4. 6th
5. 7th
6. 2nd

7. A
8. B
9. A
10. F
11. D
12. F

A) 5th
B) 4th
C) 6th
D) 5th
E) 2nd
F) 7th

INTERVAL QUALITY

1. M3
2. m2
3. m3

4. m2
5. A4
6. P5

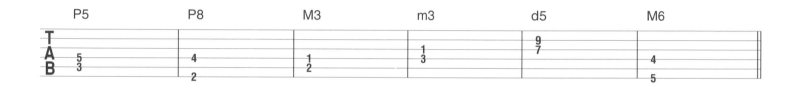

INTERVAL SHAPES

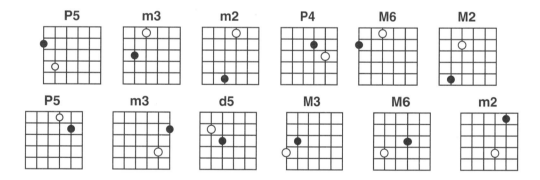

MUSICAL TERMS

Dot = Increases the duration of a note by 50 percent

Augmented = One half step larger than a major or perfect interval

Interval Quality = Determined by counting half steps

Power Chord = Another name for the harmonic interval of a perfect 5th

Pedal Tone = A note that repeats while other notes change above or below it

Harmonic Interval = Two notes sounded simultaneously

Interval Quantity = Determined by counting note letter names

CHECKPOINT 3 ANSWER KEY

TRIADS

1. 3
2. 4
3. Major, minor, augmented, diminished
4. Augmented
5. Minor
6. Diminished
7. Major

A) Em
B) G
C) C
D) D
E) Fm
F) A°
G) B
H) Em
I) Cm
J) A♭
K) F#m (or G♭m)
L) Dm

HARMONIZED MAJOR SCALE

1. Major chords, minor chords
2. 3
3. 1
4. I ii iii IV V vi vii°
5. Am
6. D
7. Dm

MUSICAL TERMS

Stacking 3rds = Building chords with a scale, using the every-other-note process

Diatonic = A note or chord belonging to the key

Root = The note after which a chord is named

Triad = A chord containing three different notes

Non-diatonic = A note or chord that doesn't belong to the key